SpringerBriefs in Law

More information about this series at http://www.springer.com/series/10164

Ondrej Hamuľák

National Sovereignty in the European Union

View from the Czech Perspective

Springer

Ondrej Hamuľák
Faculty of Law
Palacký University
Olomouc
Czech Republic

ISSN 2192-855X ISSN 2192-8568 (electronic)
SpringerBriefs in Law
ISBN 978-3-319-45350-7 ISBN 978-3-319-45351-4 (eBook)
DOI 10.1007/978-3-319-45351-4

Library of Congress Control Number: 2016949110

Printed on acid-free paper

This Springer imprint is published by Springer Nature
The registered company is Springer International Publishing AG
The registered company address is: Gewerbestrasse 11, 6330 Cham, Switzerland

Venujem Klárke a Emičke

Acknowledgments

Ondrej Hamuľák (born 1982) is Senior Lecturer in EU law at Faculty of Law, Palacký University Olomouc (Czech Republic), Visiting Professor at Tallinn Law School, TTU (Estonia) and researcher at Faculty of Law, Comenius University in Bratislava (Slovakia).

The research for this work was performed within the realisation of the project reg. no.: OPVK CZ.1.07/2.3.00/30.0041 (Podpora vytváření excelentních výzkumných týmů a intersektorální mobility na Univerzitě Palackého v Olomouci II – POST-UP II), which was financially supported by the European Social Fund and state budget of the Czech Republic.

The finalisation of the book was performed on behalf of Jean Monnet Centre of Excellence at the Faculty of Law, Palacký University Olomouc which is supported by the Jean Monnet Programme (project number 565445-EPP-1-2015-1-CZ-EPPJMO-CoE).

Contents

Chapter 1
Introduction

The process of European integration leads to a competition of power centres (Bárány 2007) and to a certain degree of multi-level governance. The European Union has to some extent become a rival to nation states, i.e. to state power. EU is being described as a specific entity 'developing from a network of treaties', surpassing in some areas its Member States and as such thus violating external aspects of their sovereignty (Klokočka 2006). At the same time, the European Union is a normative centre. It has its own independent legal system, which produces the internal effects in the Member State's practice and concurs with the national law. EU undoubtedly profiles itself as an independent entity, as some kind of a sovereign power which independently and individually manages the agenda entrusted to it by a transfer of competences from Member States.

The EU is a specific complex organism, which disposes of independent decision-making tools and own power mechanisms. It can autonomously and directly affect the legal status of legal subjects, and that makes it a form of public power, a self-governing subject, and a sovereign of its kind, which coexists with its basic units. It is worth to mention here the so called 'Gaudet-cabal'[1] articulated by the European Court of Justice (hereafter referred as Court of Justice) in one of its key rulings in case Van Gend en Loos: 'Community constitutes a new legal order of international law for the benefit of which the states have limited their sovereign rights, albeit within limited fields, and the subjects of which comprise not only the Member States but also their nationals'.[2]

The very foundation of European integration, the supranational method based on the transfer of competences from the national to the European level, is essentially programmed to limit the powers of Member States. One cannot resist the feeling

[1]Above-mentioned figure refers to Mr. Michel Gaudet, Director General of the European Commission's Legal Service and reputed author of the European Commission opinion in Van Gen den Loos case (Stein 2005).
[2]Van Gend en Loos, 26/62, ECLI:EU:C:1963:1.

O. Hamuľák, *National Sovereignty in the European Union*,
SpringerBriefs in Law, DOI 10.1007/978-3-319-45351-4_1

that European integration seems like a process of coordinated deconstruction of Member States' sovereignty.[3]

The EU ceased to be just a forum for negotiations between independent and sovereign nation states. It overlaps with the states and becomes their competitor. It is a fact that the European Union is a new normative centre which creates its own independent legal system. This law, through its normative effects and application in everyday practice, violates the autonomy of national law. Thus the traditional state's monopoly on legal violence on its own territory is no longer present.

However, despite the pressure of integration, the EU does not replace or absorb its Member States. States are still the key founding blocks of integration, with a crucial position within the processes of constitutional transformations of the EU. European integration then brings us to a Janus-faced dilemma. Apart from understanding states as building blocks of the EU, we must keep in mind the perpetual process of the autonomous constitutionalization of the European Union and the fields where it enjoys independence (own institutions, own legal system, own budgetary power, independent judicial power, autonomous and dominant legal norms, etc.).

The integration is correlated with a certain degree of constitutional tensions and debates about defining the roles of the Member States, and the role of the EU, within it. One topical question is how the integration and normative ambitions of the EU touch upon the concept of national/state sovereignty. Is the EU a quasi-federation with the sovereignty held by the centre? Or is it just a product of state's will, where sovereignty is still and only held by the Member States? Or did sovereignty disappear once the Member States opted for supranationality as the basic method of their cooperation? The participation in the integration project opens the question whether it takes away or weakens sovereignty of Member States. Or in other words whether the process of integration is State-building or State-replacing (Weatherill 2010).

In the context of European integration, the classical concept of sovereignty loses its original content and meaning. The growing importance of the European Union and the issue of its relationship with its Member States bring back the traditional discussion on the divisiveness of national sovereignty and the possibilities to manage a part of it.[4]

---

[3]The transfer of nation state competences under the umbrella of common governance has been a constant process ever since the establishment of the European Coal and Steel Community (1951), it was expressed also for example in the opening of cooperation in foreign and security policy and home affairs as established by the Maastricht Treaty (1992) or it is present in the contemporary endeavours to form a fiscal union (2012). It is actually irrelevant whether the transfer involves a supranational or intergovernmental method or their hybrid forms. Either way, the nation states are left with less autonomy in decision-making, which limits their material sovereignty.

[4]The issue of divisibility of sovereignty appears every time where there is the need to defend the existence of new social structures different from traditional nation states, and it plays no role whether these are protectorates, semi-sovereign states, federation Member States, etc. (Oppenheim 1924).

The European integration process calls for the need to newly define the contours of sovereignty of Member State in the field of constitutional law theory and theory of state. We cannot deny that membership of any country in the EU has affected its national sovereignty. The constitutional law scholars reflect the perpetually deepening integration process and open the questions to what extent is doctrine ready to present a theoretical conceptual model of theory of state that would be able to describe the unique phenomenon of the European Union? (Holländer 2009) This anticipates the need for new conceptual frameworks and theoretical moves, which would also involve the essence of national sovereignty.

The research objective of this volume is to analyze the implications of the EU membership on the understanding of national sovereignty. In particular, I am mostly interested in investigating the effects of EU membership on the concept of the national sovereignty.

I am aware of the fact, that theoretical definitions of some concepts and their real perceptions within the process of forming of social relations are not always similar and open some discrepancies. The notion of sovereignty represents one of these open, flexible concepts. It was referred that in the theoretical world, sovereignty has an absolute character, but in the world of modern politics, in relations within and among nation states, it is contested and autonomously and heteronomously limited (Povolný 1993). In order to avoid this barrier between theory and practice, I base my conclusions mainly on the analysis of the reactions of the Czech Constitutional Court (further CCC) to the various challenges of the membership of the Czech Republic in the EU.

The goal of present research volume is to present the paths of harmonization between Czech sovereign statehood (the constitutional requirement according to which 'The Czech Republic is a sovereign, unitary, and democratic state governed by the rule of law, founded on respect for the rights and freedoms of man and of citizens', article 1 paragraph 1 of the Constitution) and participation in the European integration project. I claim that the Czech Republic continues to be a sovereign country even after it joined the European Union. EU membership does not imply a loss of national sovereignty, but it requires modifications in its traditional understanding. Favouring an open concept of shared sovereignty guarantees the preservation of the national sovereignty at the ideal (theoretical) level. Above and beyond, we can simply claim that the Czech Republic is in charge. As a democratic state based on the rule of law it cannot in its very nature accept the supremacy of EU law over all national law, and so it maintains functional sovereignty in the real world of application practice.

This volume presents the following hypotheses: By joining the European Union, the Czech Republic did not lose the status of a sovereign state. Authorizing supranational institutions to exercise power over some of its original competences does not imply loss or depreciation of national sovereignty.

In order to be able to articulate above-mentioned claim, we need to accept a shift in traditional understanding of national sovereignty from a classical, static definition to a more open and dynamic concept. Despite the undeniable impact of the EU law on Czech law, the recognition of direct effect and the acceptance of its supremacy,

Czech law still shows certain basic structural elements, which are immune to the pressures of the supranational legal system. Core values of the Czech constitutional system (adhering to the indivisibility of values of a democratic state based on the rule of law even in relation to EU law) and Kompetenz-Kompetenz power of CCC, i.e. the permission to guard ultra vires conduct of EU institutions, sustain its autonomy even as an EU Member State.

In particular I put on four arguments to proof the hypothesis that Member States (and Czech Republic as used example) continues to be a sovereign countries even in realms of the membership in the European Union:

1. Sovereignty of Member State could be preserved if we skip into the new understanding of this theoretical construct while interpreting the constitutional requirements.
2. Sovereignty as the normative superiority is underlined by the constitutional claim of inviolability of core constitutional values.
3. Member States still remain in the position of Master of Treaties which gives them strong position in the future forming of European project.
4. Member States have an explicit right to withdraw from the Union so they are free to make decisions about their future 'European Destiny'.

First two of the above-mentioned claims are rather internal, i.e. national. They are based on the analysis and evaluation of the case load of CCC. It has issued a wide range of decisions regarding the conceptual comprehension of national sovereignty, relationship between the Czech and supranational law, constitutional limits of EU law applicability and about role of general and constitutional judiciary in the context of the Czech membership in the EU. The Court has acknowledged that membership in a supranational organization brings changes and challenges to the system of national law, imposes new obligations on national institutions, but in the same time that it cannot lead to a disintegration of Czech statehood.[5]

Later two arguments are rather supranational. The system of vertical relations between EU and Member States and vertical division of powers includes number of tools which increases the relevance of Member States. One may point for instance on the principle of mutual loyalty based on the article 4 TEU or possibility of the restoration of competences from the EU back to the Member States (article 48 paragraph 2 TEU in relation to primary law, declaration no. 18 of the Final Act of the IGC which adopted the Treaty of Lisbon). Among these 'state-strengthening-measures' two are of significant relevance for my claims. Possibility to model the EU by the Treaty revisions and right to withdraw from it clearly shows that Member States are still crucial building blocks of the EU.

[5]The most relevant decisions which will be widely referred hereafter in this volume are: Sugar Quotas III, Pl.ÚS 50/04, ECLI:CZ:US:2006:Pl.US.50.04; European Arrest Warrant, Pl. ÚS 66/04, ECLI:CZ:US:2006:Pl.US.66.04; Treaty of Lisbon I, Pl. ÚS 19/08, ECLI:CZ:US:2008:Pl. US.19.08.1; Treaty of Lisbon II, Pl. ÚS 29/09, ECLI:CZ:US:2009:Pl.US.29.09.3; Slovak Pensions XVII, PL. ÚS 5/12, ECLI:CZ:US:2012:Pl.US.5.12.1.

References

Bárány, E. (2007). *Pojmy dobrého práva [Notions of good law]*. Bratislava: Eurokódex.

Holländer, P. (2009). Suverenita státu (paradoxy a otazníky) [State sovereignty (paradoxes and questions)]. In A. Gerloch & J. Wintr (Eds.), *Lisabonská smlouva a ústavní pořádek ČR [Treaty of Lisbon and Czech constitutional order]* (pp. 87–114). Plzeň: Aleš Čeněk.

Klokočka, V. (2006). *Ústavní systémy evropských států [Constitutional systems of European states]*. Praha: Linde.

Oppenheim, F. L. (1924). *Mezinárodní právo [International law]*. Praha: Orbis.

Povolný, M. (1993). Nezávislost, svrchovanost a federace [Independence, sovereignty, federation]. In K. Schelle (Ed.), *Aktuální otázky českého a československého konstitucionalismu* [Actual issues of Czech and Czechoslovak constitutionalism] (pp. 68–69). Brno: Masarykova Univerzita.

Stein, E. (2005). The magic of the C-word. *EUSA Review, 18*(3), 3–4.

Weatherill, S. (2010). *Cases and Materials on EU Law*, 9th edition. Oxford: Oxford University Press.

Chapter 2
Constitutionalism Beyond the State

2.1 Supranationality as a Womb of Post-Westphalian Deconstructions

The supranational character of the European Union or supranationality itself represents a methodological basis for EU constitutionalization. This model of cooperation manifests the utilitarian and functionalist understanding of European integration, which emphasizes the efficiency of achieving the outlined goals of cooperation (Craig 1999). This concept favours decision-making and the regulation of specific activities, which are confined to an independent administration, which unlike political representation, can more rapidly and effectively react to emerging problems, and to common desires of all involved entities. The formation of supranational blocs not only helps to solve internal/mutual problems of the participating states, but later it also becomes a consolation and means of confronting the challenges of globalization (Holländer 2009).

The choice of the supranational method for the re-start of cooperation in post-war Europe was based on the suppression of the logic of sovereign equality of states—one of the basal principles of public international law.[1] Supranational

[1]This principle was articulated by the Allies as a basis of post-war order of international relations at the Moscow conference in October 1943, and after WW2 it was mentioned in the United Nations Charter (article 2 paragraph 1). States are formally equal without prejudice to real power relations and power distribution (military, economic and technical). Under sovereign equality, nation states remain sovereign actors of the international community. There is no power that would be superior to them, thus, no nation state can be forced to accept the binding effect of legal acts, which the nation state did not participate on or did not agree with. We can observe a certain paradox here. Even if we consider sovereign equality as just a different name for national sovereignty, the establishment of international institutions and organizations makes its formulation problematic, and its preservation threatens their existence. Hans Kelsen presented a contemporary (and critical) analysis of the sovereign equality principle, where he highlighted the problem of combining sovereign equality (which expected nation states to remain sovereign) with the actual practice of international organization's jurisprudence (Kelsen 1944).

O. Hamuľák, *National Sovereignty in the European Union*,
SpringerBriefs in Law, DOI 10.1007/978-3-319-45351-4_2

cooperation negates this principle by several special features. Most visible is the introduction of the qualified majority voting in the Council in connection with the general binding force of decisions for all Member States. This could lead to a situation when a Member State is bound by legal acts even if it did not vote in favour of, or even it explicitly disagreed with, which violated the formal equality of all voting countries. Furthermore, sovereign equality was affected by the establishment of an autonomous Court, which has obligatory jurisdiction in some specified areas and which is authorized to review the compliance of Member States' behaviour with the demands of supranational law. Three basal instruments which helps the Court of Justice to enforce EU law are: the judicial discourse, binding judgements, and sanction-threats specified by article 260 of the Treaty on the Functioning of the European Union (Panke 2010). Finally, the traditional position of Member States is also affected by introduction of special responsibility regime that helps to enforce obligations that stemmed from EU membership to the states—these were on one hand the doctrine of Member States' duty to pay compensation to individuals that suffered a loss due to the state's violation of EU law (Aalto 2011) as well as introduction of the special judicial procedure concerning the breaches of EU law by the Member States—infringement procedure according to article 258 TFEU—where Commission (as representative of supranational power) serves as the main prosecutor.

As a result, the supranational organization competes with its forming blocs—the national states. The EU is perceived as a mixed structure surpassing the definition of a traditional international organization, and combining features of federation and confederation—it has jurisdiction and the power to legal regulation in certain areas in all EU Member States; it uses the concept of divided competences of Member States (units) and the EU (whole); it has the contractual foundations and holds the subjectivity; and it has an autonomous set of own institutions (Wintr 2004). European Communities and later European Union hold a sufficient autonomy and space to comprehensively and without interference of Member States (or occasionally even without their approval) manage affairs falling under its competences. The supranational organization—a legal subject separate and independent of its founding members—is positioned to certain extent 'above' its Member States. This 'superiority' towards Member States manifests itself in all stages of the law-making process, and in the process of application of EU law. As a result, the law-making institutions are independent, they have autonomous decision-making powers, they independently execute individual decisions and accomplish objectives, which they have defined, and finally EU law affects the legal status of individuals, who can be awarded the rights or prescribed duties based on a supranational legal regulation (Lenaerts and Van Nuffel 2005). The European Union is endowed with a comprehensive institutional, political and legal system, which likens it to a state and represents a constitutional framework for its operation.

The supranational impetus associated with the creation of European Communities and the evolution of the integration leads us to some theoretical assumptions according to which international law in European region has entered into post-Westphalian period (MacCormick 1999; Jakab 2006). This means the necessity of rejection of the classical conception of the state sovereignty (indivisible, exclusive, highest power) and acceptance of some supranational political and legal will. I pay further attention to this phenomenon in the next chapters of this volume.

European integration is something like planed and controlled deconstruction of the content of the sovereignty of Member States. This phenomenon then logically opens the debate about the nature of European Union itself. The central point of this debate is the question whether the European Union is on the track to be a state-like organization? I am not going to claim that European Union is a 'super-state' which replaced or is replacing the Member States. But on the other side one have to accept that European Union is an autonomous entity, the original political structure which has its own efficient construction of the internal organization and distinctive goals and instruments leading to them.

2.2 The Complex Story of EU Constitutionalization

European integration transfers authority from Member States towards the supranational centre (Agnew 2009). This is the main building bloc of EU's own constitutional story. Why do I speak about a story rather than a system? I believe that the term 'story' better describes the specifics of the EU integration model, its openness, constant changes, and doctrinal un-restrictiveness. EU constitutionalization and its constitutional matrix might be better understood as a narrative rather than an exact formula. The story is a complex phenomenon. Here, the term complexity manifests itself in both its linguistic meanings[2]; referring to its complicated internal structure (involving many different related fragments), and to certain level of incomprehensibility, which makes our understanding of this phenomenon more intricate. The constitutionalization of the European project has certain quantitative dimension (formal constitutional law)—its structures, systems of operation, and performed duties are constantly closer to the systems of the inner organization of nation states (Forejtová 2011). But it has also some qualitative dimension (material constitutional law) while it is acquiring a constitutional character in terms of a system of governance respecting rule of law, democratic principles and the inviolability of an individual's personal spheres. A large variety of texts examining EU constitutionality almost unanimously assume that its basis lies in some autonomous, internally organized structure of norms, relationships and principles without the existence of a written constitution (Weiler 1999; Rosas and Armati 2010).

The unique characteristic of the Union gives rise to the notion of constitutional movement which accompanies the European integration. 'Constitutionality', 'Constitutional Law', 'Constitutional System'—all these terms currently exceeds

[2]See the entry 'complex' in the online version of Cambridge English Dictionary (http://dictionary.cambridge.org/dictionary/british/).

beyond the borders of national states (De Búrca and Weiler 2012) and thus cannot be regarded as sole objectives of the national law and jurisprudence. Certainly there is no classical original pouvoir constituant behind the creation of the European Union. But this claim does not contest the fact that the integration entities display characteristics of a distinct constitutional system. The evidence of existence of such system may be found in the specific structural elements that differentiates the European Union from the traditional international organizations.

We may find the social/institutional, normative and also material/meta-legal arguments in favour of assertion that European Union has its own substantive Constitution.

European Union has its own internal organization of relations between main participating players (European Union and its Member States), between institutions of the Union and between Union and the individuals/citizens of the Union. Here the assertion of material constitutionality should sound like this: Where autonomous society exists, i.e. some political and societal structure, there is a Constitution. The classic Latin maxim *Ubi societas ibi ius* is transferred to the constitutional level here. This approach to the material meaning of constitution is adhered to the theory of state of Georg Jellinek.

Another point is connected with the ability of the Union to manifest its own will by the adoption of law (Forejtová and Tronecková 2011) and making of administrative decisions. The Union has its own independent legal framework that lays down rules of adoption of binding provisions. These provisions express the Union powers in the outer world and they are internally applicable within the Member States practice. The autonomous legal system give rise to the Kelsen's argument which should sound like this: Where a law is present, i.e. autonomous legal system is working, there is a Constitution.

The last argument is connected with allegation according to which, where a rule of law (i.e. democratic system based on the rule of law and protection of the fundamental rights) is respected there is a Constitution. Here, the role of mechanisms of promotion and respecting the fundamental rights is crucial without any doubts.

The key role in determining the contours of the constitutionality of the European Union was and still is played by the Court of Justice of the European Union. The Court supported its quest for understanding the EU law as an autonomous constitutional system also by some semantic turnovers. In judgment *Les Verts*[3] or *Opinion on the EEA Treaty*[4] it expressly referred to the Treaty as constitutional charter of the integration entities (Lenaerts 2010). It repeated this argument and the crucial requirement which rises from it (that the [Union] is based on the rule of law, inasmuch as neither its Member States nor its institutions can avoid review of the conformity of their acts with the basic constitutional charter, the Treaty) also in more recent constitutional 'hard cases' *Kadi*[5] and *Opinion on Agreement on*

[3]Les Verts v Parliament, 294/83, ECLI:EU:C:1986:166.

[4]Opinion on the EEA Treaty, 1/91, ECLI:EU:C:1991:490.

[5]Kadi and Al Barakaat International Foundation v Council and Commission, C-402/05 P and C-415/05 P, ECLI:EU:C:2008:461.

Accession to the ECHR.[6] The Court of Justice furthermore promoted independence and some practical domination of European Union law as a prerequisite for the functionality of the entire project of European integration. It served as the agent of emancipation of supranational law and supranational entities.[7] And it was the Court itself who played the pioneer role within the notion of respecting the fundamental rights as general principles within the supranational legal and political structure (de Witte 1999).

It is a fact that European Union lacks a written constitution. The attempt for its 'documentary constitutionalisation'[8] connected with the draft Treaty Establishing a Constitution of Europe has failed.[9] Notwithstanding that the theory of EU law and the Court of Justice does use the term 'constitution/constitutional Charter' without any doubts. EU is a sovereign polity with its own (even though not specifically designated) constitution, because it has its own system of legal rules, which regulate its objectives, institutional competences, and individual rights, while establishing the nature of the relationship between the centre, i.e. EU and its units, i.e. Member States (Leczykiewicz 2009). Having in mind the complex sum of arguments mentioned above the existence of the Constitutional system of the European Union is a hardly contestable phenomenon. Of course it goes about the constitutionality in the substantive sense of the word, the constitutionality based on principles, a separation of powers and the human rights protection system, i.e. a respected constitutionality and not one which was formally enacted or literally stated.

2.3 The Democratic Arrangement of the Internal Functioning of the EU

The constitutional system and the constitutional law of the European Union predict the existence of fundamental rules of organization of social structures. It indicates that the Union may be foreseen as a legal community, an equivalent of the rule of law-based state. It is a constitutional structure of a kind which acts, behaviours and is regulated by the set of rules which have its own democratic ethos. The biggest

[6]Opinion on the Agreement on Accession of the European Union to the European Convention for the Protection of Human Rights and Fundamental Freedoms, 2/13, ECLI:EU:C:2014:2454.

[7]This is playing the role of "Constitutional Court of the European Union." See Lenaerts and Van Nuffel (2011, p. 22).

[8]A term used to describe the process of drafting and adopting of the Treaty Establishing a Constitution of Europe by Matej Avbelj and Jan Komárek (Avbelj and Komárek 2012).

[9]Treaty Establishing a Constitution of Europe was prepared between February 2002 and July 2003. It was signed by all Member States during an intergovernmental conference in June 2004. As well known, the ratification process ended after it was rejected by a referendum in France and the Netherlands (2005).

shift towards democratic symbolism is connected with the Lisbon reform of primary law. Restructuring the EU, or rather its internal unification and simplification, represents the historically largest broadening of the EU's material competences. Apart from the significant changes such as the unification of the Union's pillar structure, gaining legal subjectivity to the EU and general simplification of the integration entities by replacing the Community with a Union, the Treaty of Lisbon introduced many changes and novelties, which aimed at further establishing the supranational character of the EU, strengthening its legitimacy in the eyes of the internal subjects, i.e. Member States and individuals, increasing the effectiveness of the decision-making process, securing internal security of the Union, and increasing its importance in the international arena (Craig 2010).

The arrangement of the EU after Lisbon further strengthens the supranational elements of integration. The most systemic factors in this regard (which lead towards central governance, politically unify the EU and support its federal tendencies) are: the new system of division of competences (article 2–3 TFEU), introduction of the so-called passerelle clause (article 48 paragraph 7 TEU) or the extension of applicability in case of the flexibility clause (article 352 TFEU).

Other features increase the democratic legitimacy and accountability of the EU and strengthen the ties between EU and individuals. Treaty of Lisbon made binding the Charter of Fundamental Rights of the EU (article 6 TEU), which comprises the list of fundamental rights that the EU and its Member States must respect. The Treaty anticipated the citizen's initiative (article 11 paragraph 4 TEU). It strengthened the role of national parliaments which started to serve as control points within the so-called early warning system in respect to fulfilment of the principle of subsidiarity (Kiiver 2012) and of the European Parliament, which became an equal partner of the Council through the introduction of the ordinary legislative procedure for secondary law adoption, article 288 TFEU. Besides that the simplification of the rules for the access of individuals to justice (by widening the locus standi of individuals in the connection with the action for annulment according to article 263 TFEU) broadened the competences (or control potential) of the Court of Justice (Mazák 2011).

There were also some ideological features of the shift towards more legitimate and democratic Union. They are first of all expressed in the definition of values that the EU's activities should observe as specified in article 2 TEU: 'The Union is founded on the values of respect for human dignity, freedom, democracy, equality, the rule of law and respect for human rights, including the rights of persons belonging to minorities. These values are common to the Member States in a society in which pluralism, non-discrimination, tolerance, justice, solidarity and equality between women and men prevail'.

The demarcation of the democratic values of the EU completes the EU's value basis. These democratic values are defined by Title II TEU and they include the equality of EU's citizens, representative democracy, dialogue with civil society, and a principle, which we could describe as decentralization of the decision-making processes, which rests on the amplified role and wider competences of national parliaments. The accentuation of values and principles underlines the state-like character/ambitions of the EU. It is not surprising that EU is getting the label as 'partially federal entity' (Piris 2010).

It is often assumed that a serious effort to federalize supranational entities must be accompanied with an adequate increase in their democratic legitimacy (Habermas 2001). The authors of the last major reform of the primary law (Constitutional treaty and its Lisbon 'clone') to a large extent satisfied these calls and (according to Habermasian logic[10]) made another step towards federalizing the EU. Even though there are some critical voices (Mac Amhlaigh 2011) it is clear that Treaty of Lisbon certainly increases the democratic legitimacy of both input democracy, i.e. shift towards parliamentarianism and output democracy, i.e. respecting rights of individuals (Lenaerts and Cambien 2009). When we take into account that identification of basic values, higher importance of Union's citizenship (Forejtová 2014) or the increased role of national parliaments (article 12 TEU) enhanced the traditional supranational features (especially the triad: autonomous competences—autonomous institutions—autonomous law), we must accept that the EU has fortified the legitimacy of its existence and activities, and is headed towards deeper federalization of Europeans, therefore it is in accordance to Jean Monnet's programming statement (presented in Washington, 30 April 1952): '*Nous ne coalisons pas des États, nous unissons des hommes*'.

2.4 Coven of Lawyers and Its Child—Emancipated and Dominant EU Law

2.4.1 New Legal System Shaped by Judges and Lawyers

The nature of European Community and today European Union law has been essentially connected with the supranational nature of European integration. Meeting the autonomous objectives of integration requires an autonomous, effective and unified legal system. A new lawmaker other than a nation state unavoidably emerged here. Ability to regulate the behaviour and conduct of society abandoned the exclusive monopoly of state power and thus opened way for a pluralistic set-out (Bárány 2007).

Yet, we have to note that the creation of European Communities had an international legal (contractual) basis and as such EC law was originally considered as a part of the public international law. The authors of the Treaties did not try or did not need to resolve the challenges of use and effects of EC law within the national legal systems. Nor they shaped the relationship between EC and national law or established the procedures for resolving the potential conflict. They tacitly assumed that these issues would be resolved by the constitutional law of the Member States

[10]Jürgen Habermas belongs among the most powerful advocates of the need to increase the EU's legitimacy (Habermas 2001).

(access to the international legal commitments, theories of dualism and monism, the concept of national law's precedence over international law) or alternatively by the concepts of public international law (the concept of a self-executing international treaty).

Thus, the Treaties do not include any specific instructions on how to use the EC/EU law in national practice and how its relationship to national law must be settled.[11] The Court of Justice played an irreplaceable role here as it became to serve as the engine of shaping the character of EU law and as pivotal authority marking the line between supranational and national law. It is worth mentioning the fact that the Court of Justice actually seized this position despite the weak and unclear definition of its competences in the EU primary law which was referred as 'fragile jurisdictional base' (Stein 1981). Mainly thanks to the Court of Justice that the process of EU law constitutionalization took place (Corrias 2011). Jiří Přibáň adds that the utopia of European (supranational) constitutionalization could materialize only owing to this specific group of lawyers working for the Court of Justice and in the legal services of the other Community institutions (Přibáň 2010). Eric Stein described the importance of the lawyers' estate for the deepening of European integration with the following hyperbole (paraphrased in the title of this chapter): 'Constitutionalisation of European integration is a story of a dark conspiracy and outrageous collusion, engineered by a coven of judges and lawyers against unsuspecting governments' (Stein 2005).

2.4.2 Autonomous Legal System

The nature of the European Union law is necessarily interconnected with the supranational character of the European integration. In order to achieve autonomous objectives of the integration entities an autonomous, effective and uniform legal order is required.

The Court of Justice gradually defined the EC/EU law as an autonomous legal order valid within the territory of all Member States (Stein 1981) It has laid down that this law is directly applicable without the need of its reception into the national legal orders. Its internal effects are independent from principles of legal orders of Member States; far from it the supranational law itself via its own application principles defines its internal effects within the legal orders of Member States.

The fundamental characteristic of the European Union legal order is its independence, sometimes recalled as sovereignty of EU law (Jacobs 2007). It means that this legal order exists independently from the national law of Member States and general public international law. It is a legal order different from both international and national law and it has an autonomous character defined by these elementary features (Barents 2004).

---

[11]The only exception was the explicit definition of direct effect as a source of secondary law.

- Own constitutional basis laid down in founding Treaties, i.e. rules of law with a constitutional character which concern only the European Union. 'The European Economic Community is based on the rule of law, neither its Member States nor its institutions can avoid a review of the question whether the measures adopted by them are in conformity with the basic constitutional charter, the Treaty'(*Les Verts*[12]).
- The existence of the Court of Justice as its own, autonomous court of last instance that interprets the EU law. The Community law has the only one binding interpretation and this interpretation is exclusively made by the Court of Justice who has this exclusive competence (*Krohn*[13]). The same exclusive competence applies considering the validity of rules of the European Union law. This competence is conferred only upon the Court of Justice (*Foto-Frost*[14]). National courts are in case of doubts about the validity of rules of the European Union law entitled to bring a preliminary question to the Court of Justice. However, they cannot decide whether the rule of EU law is valid or not themselves.
- The completeness and self-sufficiency of the European Union law required to solve issues under the competences of the European Union (especially the sphere of exclusive competences) reflects that in order to achieve effects presumed by the EU law no law-making activity from the national institutions of Member States is required.
- Autonomous determination of the characteristics and the principles of application of supranational law. These principles are based on the case law of the Court of Justice which determines the conditions of their use. National legal orders do not regulate these principles specifically.

The Court of Justice pointed out in its case law that even though the Communities were established by an international treaty and thus they derived from the public international law, they cannot be regarded as typical international organizations. Nor their legislation is a regional public international law, but a legal order with specific characteristics. 'The Community constitutes a new legal order of international law for the benefit of which the states have limited their sovereign rights, albeit within limited fields, and the subjects of which comprise not only Member States but also their nationals' (*Van Gend en Loos*[15]). In less than a year and a half after the Van Gend en Loos case the Court of Justice make the supranational law absolutely independent from the international public law and defined as a completely independent (autonomous) legal order. 'The EEC treaty has created its own legal system which, on the entry into force of the treaty, became an integral part of the legal systems of the Member States and which their courts are bound to apply' (*Costa vs. ENEL*[16]).

[12]Les Verts v Parliament, 294/83, ECLI:EU:C:1986:166.

[13]Krohn, 74/69, ECLI:EU:C:1970:58.

[14]Foto-Frost, 314/85, ECLI:EU:C:1987:452.

[15]Van Gend en Loos, 26/62, ECLI:EU:C:1963:1.

[16]Costa vs. ENEL, 6/64, ECLI:EU:C:1964:66.

The autonomous character of the Union law is logically followed by a certain 'self-enforceability' of this law within the territory of the Member States. That means that the Member States are not anymore supposed to make their own decisions regarding the internal effects of the European Union law. The traditional monist and dualist theory that defines the system of internal effects and applicability of the international law rules within the national legal orders, does not apply here. In contrast to that traditional view the European Union law defines its effects autonomously; it prescribes the kind of EU monism (Forejtová 2015). By making the supranational law 'independent', the Court of Justice refuted the schematic opinion that the EC law was just another form of international law and its subjects could be only contractual parties (e.g. national states). The penetration of supranational law into the national legal systems disrupts the 'sovereignty idol'—the traditional concept according to which a direct intervention of supranational (international) norms into the legal system of a sovereign country is inadmissible (Klokočka 2006). The tensions between revolutionary and traditional approach was visible also during 'negotiating' the landmark decision in Van Gend en Loos case, where three of the opposing Member States (Germany, Belgium, and the Netherlands) unsuccessfully contended against self-enforceability of supranational law by argument that sovereignty had to be preserved.

The main effect is that European Union law prescribes the obligation (recalled as 'duty to apply'; see Prechal 2007) of national authorities to use its provisions directly without any need to adopt implementing national rules = the principle of the direct applicability. The European Union law is an independent legal order but in a meantime it 'is an integral part' of the legal order applicable in the territory of each of the Member States (*Simmenthal*[17]).

According to the Court of Justice, the direct (immediate) applicability means that the provisions of the European Union law shall be applied uniformly and fully from the date of their entry into force for so long as they will be set aside. The Court of Justice makes in this connection no differences between the Union law and the national law regarding their application by the national courts and public authorities. On the contrary, it recognizes the provisions of the European Union law as an inseparable part of the legal orders of the Member States 'The direct applicability of Community law means that its rules must be fully and uniformly applied in all the Member States from the date of their entry into force and for so long as they continue in force. Directly applicable provisions are a direct source of rights and duties for all those affected thereby, whether Member States or individuals; this consequence also concerns any national court whose task it is as an organ of a Member State to protect the rights conferred upon individuals by community law' (*Simmenthal*).

The courts and even the administrative authorities (*Constanzo*[18]) of the Member States are obliged to recognize the European Union law as a part of their national

[17]Simmenthal, 106/77, ECLI:EU:C:1978:49.

[18]Fratelli Constanzo, 103/88, ECLI:EU:C:1989:256.

legal order. The supranational law has become a part of the routine legal practice of the national authorities (especially the courts). The courts of the Member States were given a new power. The conferral of liability of application and enforcement of the rules of supranational law upon national courts makes them a part of the 'general judicial system of the Union'. Wide responsibility of the national general courts led to increase of their importance and fuels the changes in their relation to the national Constitutional Court (Komárek 2014).

Direct (immediate) application of European Union law is a crucial element of its autonomy. In essence it includes the command to national courts to acknowledge the supranational law as the law of their 'own land' and apply it in the forms in which it was originally adopted by the supranational power, i.e. without the need to transpose it into intrastate sources. The impact here is objective and abstract.

However, independence of EU law also embraces a subjective/personal dimension. It directly addresses individuals through the so-called direct effect principle. Direct effect means that the provisions of EU law are capable to create rights and impose duties for the individual subjects of national law, i.e. natural and legal persons. Direct effect makes EU law a direct source of influencing the legal status of legal subjects at a national level. Awarding the EU legal norms with direct effect principle significantly enhanced the rules of effective applicability of EU law and boosted individuals' status in the legal system.

The Court of Justice's case law regarding direct effect and especially as far as the secondary law was concerned was based on the need for efficiency and utility of supranational norms. The so-called 'l'effet utille' requirement (Sehnálek 2009) would have been significantly undermined if the Member States failed to meet the obligations imposed on them by the EU rules.

Effective functioning of the EU legal system requires Member States, as carriers of specific duties to be continuously supervised. This supervision is primarily executed by the Commission, which can take a Member State to court for failure to comply with EU law (article 258 TFEU). Owing to the direct effect of EU norms, individuals also have some power to monitor the state and claim a remedy before national courts. In this respect, we talk about the so-called dual vigilance (Weatherill 2010) or double control over the Member States. The acceptance of the direct effect of EU law gave individuals more protection and simultaneously they became protectors ('guardians') of the EU law and its integrity (Weiler 1991). The inclusion of individuals under umbrella of supranational law transformed the EU law into an absolute, complete legal system. Wide direct effect changed our perception of supranational law. EU law is built on the shoulders of individuals and individuals became the spine of its development. The presence of individuals in the EU legal order further improved our understanding of this legal system as state-like structure.

2.4.3 *Dominant Legal System*

The Court of Justice gradually defined EC (EU) law as an independent legal system valid on the territory of all Member States. It stated that this law in all its forms (e.g. the Treaties formed by the Member States, international treaties adopted by the EU itself and sources of secondary law formed by EU institutions) shall be directly applicable without the need of transposition into national legal systems. Its internal effects were not dependent on the existence of legal basis prescribed by the Member States' legal systems.

National authorities hold a number of duties vis-á-vis EU law norms. They must accept EU law as an integral part of their national legal system; they have to consider the content of EU law and objectives of the EU when interpreting national norms; and when they face the conflict between EU law and national law norms, they are under duty to give preference to the EU law norm and refuse to apply the national one. The principles of the internal application of EU law in the Member states clearly demonstrate that the notion of 'self-enforceability' of EU law should be understood in broad meaning. It is not only an ability to produce legal effect without the transposition to national system but also general dominance over national law which must be accepted here. The dominance of EU law over national law has three limbs

(a) it is capable to regulate legal situation directly despite the existence of conflicting national rule (principle of primacy);
(b) it influences and changes the interpretation and understanding of national norms (indirect effect);
(c) and it is connected with the threat of responsibility regime, i.e. risk of erase of state liability for damages caused by the serious breaches of EU law requirements by the national authorities.

If the wording or meaning of national law provisions collides with the EU law, it is the supranational law which behaves as dominant legal system. It prevails over national rules in two ways. It paralyses the applicability of conflicting national rules (*Costa* case impact) or narrows the possible ways of interpretation of national norms to only those options which are in line with the EU law requirements (*Von Colson* case impact).[19]

2.4.3.1 The Cohabitation of Colliding Legal Worlds—The Principle of Primacy of the European Union Law

The relationship between EU law and the law of the Member States is mostly determined by the primacy of former over the later. The so-called primacy of EU

[19] Von Colson and Kamann vs. Land Nordrhein-Westfalen, 14/83, ECLI:EU:C:1984:153.

law (sometimes known as supremacy[20]) belongs among the basic characteristics of EU law, and is an indispensably interconnected with the direct applicability principle.[21] A unitary application of supranational law demands that it is utilized despite conflicting national norms. TEU demarcates loyalty as a basic EU Member States' duty, according to which their activities cannot endanger EU objectives (article 4 TEU), but such vaguely defined commitment to their loyalty does not necessarily affect the autonomy of the national decision-makers will. Formal preservation of the autonomous position of the national decision-maker might be reflected in the existence of a legal norm that would collide with the EU law. The primacy principle solves such situations.

The application of this principle in real life gives the national judge (or any other authority applying the law such as administrative body, see *Constanzo* case) the obligation to abstain in the procedure in question from the application of a national norm, which contradicts the EU law and to apply the EU norm.

The establishments of the primacy principle resolves the conflict between the EU norm and the national one, because the national judge and every other national institution must in such a situation apply the EU legal norm, and ignore the conflicting national norm notwithstanding its legal nature and authority.

The primacy of the European Union law is its fundamental element that defines the relationship between this law and the national law of the Member States (Alter 2001). This principle causes that the national judge (or any other authority applying law) is (in cases decided by him) subject to an obligation not to apply the national legal rule inconsistent with the European legislation. European Union law thus enjoys the ability to take priority over national legal norms in the sphere of the judicial or administrative practice. It had to be pointed here, that primacy does not mean absolute normative superiority. Introduction of this principle into the practice

[20]The theoretical approach includes opinions which believe that primacy and supremacy should be distinguished. These opinions generally refer to the crucial judgement of the Spanish constitutional court on the compatibility of the Treaty Establishing a Constitution for Europe with the Spanish Constitution of 13 December 2004. The Constitutional Court drew a line between primacy and supremacy and accepted the former as an important characteristic of the EU law, and the latter as inherent to the norms of the Spanish Constitution, because only the Constitution contained the legal basis for Spain's EU membership. Similarly, they referred to the England and Wales High Court decision *Thoburn v Sunderland City* Council [2002] EWHC 195 (Admin), where supremacy had been connected with the constitutional basis of the EU law's effect, and primacy with actual dominance of EU law within such system (Avbelj 2011).

[21]The theory of EU law discusses whether primacy and direct applicability/direct effect are independent and separate principles of EU law, which are not necessarily related, or whether they are related where primacy acts as a rule on a conflict of norms in case when a directly applicable norm of EU law collides with national law (Hinarejos 2008). I personally prefer the latter view. The primacy principle was created to resolve conflicts between national and European law. In order for a conflict to arise, the normative spheres (Bobek et al. 2011) of EU and national law must overlap, which is possible only where there is a directly applicable EU norm. Primacy then serves as an auxiliary principle, which should help to reach the full efficacy of EU law in cases when directly applicable norm 'contradicts' the national law.

of application of law was not followed by the building of hierarchy pyramid between the European Union law and national law of Member States.

The TEU defines only the fundamental obligation of states not to jeopardize the attainment of the Union's objective = the principle of loyalty (article 4 paragraph 3 TEU). This generally defined obligation does not in principle impinge on the autonomy of the will of the national legislator. The formal preservation of the autonomous position of the national lawmaker may find it is echo in the existence of the national legislation inconsistent with the EU law. The principle of primacy was established in order to solve the collision between the supranational law and the national law. In case of this collision the national judge shall use the rule of EU law and not apply the national provisions.

The principle of primacy does not emanate directly from any text of primary or secondary law source.[22] Its basis, extent and effects were built from the case law of the Court of Justice of the European Union.

The key-decision was the judgment of the Court of Justice in *Costa* case. The Court of Justice laid down in this decision the basis of the doctrine of the primacy of the Community (now EU) law over the national law. It defined the independence of the supranational law, solved the issue of the relationship between the national law of the Member States and the Community law and the division of powers between the Union and the Member States. The Court of Justice considered the conferral of powers upon the Community/Union as permanent and definitive and recognized thus the independence of the supranational entity. According to the Court of Justice: 'By creating a community of unlimited duration, having its own institutions, its own personality, its own legal capacity and capacity of representation on the international plane and, more particularly, real powers stemming from a limitation of sovereignty or a transfer of powers from the states to the community, the Member States have limited their sovereign rights, albeit within limited fields, and have thus created a body of law which binds both their nationals and

[22]The first attempt to stipulate this relationship occurred with the drawing up of the Treaty establishing a Constitution for Europe, which for the first time stated in article I-6 the legal specifications of the EU law's primacy. The failure of the constitutional process led to a postponement of the legal definition of the EU law in the EU's primary law. The opportunity to solve this problem opened again with the Treaty of Lisbon. It is well known that this document lacked the formal constitutional ambitions of the Constitutional Treaty, thus, its text lacked provisions with constitutional symbolism and did not carry any constitutional legal implications as had been the case with article I-6 of the Constitutional Treaty. The authors of the Lisbon reform referred to the principle of primacy only in the declarations attached to the Final Act of the Intergovernmental Conference. Specifically Declaration no. 17 recalls in a form of some 'softlaw' (Craig and De Búrca 2011) that the primacy principle is a stable principle of EU law and the failure to legally define it does not change the fact that it plays an important role when securing the effective operation of EU legal regulation (The Declaration concerning primacy stipulates that: 'The Conference recalls that, in accordance with well settled case law of the Court of Justice of the European Union, the Treaties and the law adopted by the Union on the basis of the Treaties have primacy over the law of Member States, under the conditions laid down by the said case law.'). The Declaration concerning primacy can be understood as a political 'consecration' of the Court of Justice's established case law (Niedobitek 2009).

themselves. [...] the law stemming from the treaty, an independent source of law, could not, because of its special and original nature, be overridden by domestic legal provisions, however framed, without being deprived of its character as community law and without the legal basis of the community itself being called into question'.

The primacy of the European Union law is a logical supplement to the principle of the direct applicability. The uniform application of the supranational law requires necessarily applying this law despite the collision with national provisions.

The principle of primacy of the EU law covers all sources of the European Union law including the secondary legislation (*Kreil*[23]). According to the case law of the Court of Justice, the supranational law has both retroactive effects (the application of the already existing national legislation is ruled out) and future effects (the application of the new national law is ruled out in the extent they will be inconsistent with the European norms *Simmenthal*). This effect of the primacy principle derives from the requirement of an effective and uniform application of the European Union law.

The formation of the primacy doctrine in *Costa* case represented the fundamental basis within the framework of relationship between the Community (nowadays Union) legal order and the national law of the Member States. In above-mentioned case the Court of Justice did not express any limits of the primacy. Therefore, some open questions remained. The most important and the most sensitive question was whether this doctrine should apply also in connection with the cases of collision between EU law and the highest rules of the national law = the Constitution and the Constitutional law. The Court issued its opinion on this question in the judgment *Internationale Handelsgesellschaft.*[24] There it defined the absolute weight of the doctrine of primacy of the Union law. In case where the supranational law and the national constitutional provisions regulate certain issues differently, the European Union law shall prevail. National constitutional rules can't have the precedence over the European Union law. Otherwise the autonomous character of the Union and its legal order would be interfered as well as the effectiveness of achieving the objectives of integration would be impinged. The next quoted passage from that case became legendary: 'Recourse to the legal rules or concepts of national law in order to judge the validity of measures adopted by the institutions of the community would have an adverse effect on the uniformity and efficacy of community law. The validity of such measures can only be judged in the light of community law. In fact, the law stemming from the treaty, an independent source of law, cannot because of its very nature be overridden by rules of national law, however framed, without being deprived of its character as community law and without the legal basis of the community itself being called in question. Therefore the validity of a community measure or its effect within a Member State cannot be affected by allegations that it

[23]Kreil, C-285/98, ECLI:EU:C:2000:2.

[24]Internationale Handelsgesellschaft, 11/70, ECLI:EU:C:1970:114.

runs counter to either fundamental rights as formulated by the constitution of that state or the principles of a national constitutional structure'.

It is clear that Court of Justice understands primacy in absolute terms and does not distinguishes between situations where obstacles to EU law have their roots in general or constitutional law of Member state. This, however, does not change the fact that primacy principle still has more or less procedural character and the Court of Justice did not establish formal hierarchical relations between supranational and national law. There is no hierarchy between these systems in terms of the validity of norms, but there is some kind of structural relationship in terms of the applicability of concrete legal rules to the facts in particular case. The primacy of EU law simply establishes the obligations of national authorities to follow immediately the EU norms, i.e. to abstain from applying a colliding national norm in a specific procedure. A national court that hears the case cannot initiate any validity review; propose annulment or any other process of eliminating a national norm that contradicts the EU legislation. The Court of Justice specifically states that 'any provision of a national legal system and any legislative, administrative or judicial practice which might impair the effectiveness of Community law by withholding from the national court having jurisdiction to apply such law the power to do everything necessary at the moment of its application to set aside national legislative provisions which might prevent, even temporarily, Community rules from having full force and effect are incompatible with those requirements, which are the very essence of Community law.'[25]

The Court of Justice recalled the separated understanding of European and national law also in decision *Filipiak,*[26] where it is restated that: 'Pursuant to the principle of the primacy of Community law, a conflict between a provision of national law and a directly applicable provision of the Treaty is to be resolved by a national court applying Community law, if necessary by refusing to apply the conflicting national provision, and not by a declaration that the national provision is invalid, the powers of authorities, courts and tribunals in that regard being a matter to be determined by each Member State (point 82)' and further '[...] the incompatibility with Community law of a subsequently adopted rule of national law does not have the effect of rendering that rule of national law non-existent. [...]'[27]

While it is true that the principle of the primacy of European Union law may influence in some way the decisions of the national legislature, the immediate invalidation of the national law does not follow from this principle. The question of validity or invalidity does not arise here as the two legal systems—EU law and the national law—are separate and autonomous legal orders.[28] No Treaty provision

[25]Simmenthal, 106/77, ECLI:EU:C:1978:49, point 22.

[26]Filipiak, C-314/08, ECLI:EU:C:2009:719.

[27]Filipiak, C-314/08, ECLI:EU:C:2009:719, points 82–83.

[28]The only exception where setting aside (invalidation) of conflicting national rules is necessary (or better said required by EU law) arises in the situation when even the mere existence of the national legal rule may endanger the application of the Union competences. Under those circumstances in order to strengthen the legal certainty and the position of individuals enjoying the

provides for a power to decide on the validity of national law with derogative effects. Even condemnatory decision of the Court of Justice within the infringement proceedings (article 260 TFEU) stating the failure to comply with EU legislation caused by the existence of national legislation contradicting EU law does not bring this consequences. Neither decision within preliminary ruling where the Court of Justice indirectly (commenting on an EU law provision) identifies a contradiction between national and EU norms does not have this effects.[29]

Introduction of principle of primacy and its absolute understanding vis-á-vis national constitutional law serve as one of the main arguments in federalization debate in Europe. The primacy (supremacy) of federal law over the law of the states serves as the classical constitutional arrangement of modern federal states. It should be recognized also as feature of formal constitutionalization of the EU (Schütze 2014). But it is the contested feature because this federal matrix is not explicitly regulated in the main constituent documents (the Treaties) which content the expressed will of founders—the Member States. It is only the adjudicated principle which is therefore open to (judicial) deliberations and contestations on the side of national courts, which we will see on the Czech example in second part of this volume.

2.4.3.2 Indirect Dominance of Supranational Rules. An EU-Consistent Interpretation of National Law

The EU law is capable to affect the legal practice within the Member States even much broader than by the normative influence described above. The consequences of Member State's EU membership include also the commitment to solidarity or loyalty (see article 4 paragraph 3 TEU) which stands as the building block of all non-normative (i.e. different to direct applicability of EU norms) impacts of the EU law. The most widely used non-normative impact is related to the so-called principle of indirect effect. This principle implies the obligation of national authorities to reflect the aims of EU law and to follow the goals of EU norms when interpreting national law. EU law stands here as a dominant matrix and forces the national authorities to choose the pro-European options of given possible mods of national law interpretation. Indirect effect of EU law is a flexible principle. It produces

(Footnote 28 continued)

subjective rights steaming from EU law provisions, the Member States may be obliged to eliminate (invalidate) the contradicting national rule (see *Commission v. France*, 167/73, ECLI:EU:C:1974:35). But this consequence cannot be regarded as the impact of the primacy principle. The extraordinary duty to set aside provision(s) of national law under above-mentioned circumstances must be understood as impact of general principle (obligation) of loyalty (established by article 4 paragraph 3 TEU) according to which Member States he Member States hold a duty to take all appropriate measure to ensure fulfilment of their obligations arising out of the Treaties or from the acts of the institutions of the EU.

[29]Attanasio Group, C-384/08, ECLI:EU:C:2010:133, point 16.

several consequences in national practice which are dependent on the wording and strength of EU law norm (used as the model) and wording and scope of national rule as well. EU law may be used as argument in different forms:

- as confirmative argument to underline the relevance of the chosen decision, which clearly flows from national law,
- as mediatory argument where EU norm determines which of plausible paths of interpretation of national law must be chosen.
- as evolutive argument where EU law bent the traditional interpretation of national norm and open it for new non-established meanings.[30]

The foundations of the principle of the indirect effect of the European Union law, i.e. the obligation to interpret the national law in conformity with the EU law requirements were settled in *Von Colson* case. It represents another pillar of effective impact of EU law in proceedings before national authorities. Basically it means that the national judge (or another authority responsible for application of law) is obligated to interpret the national law in the light of objectives and content of rules of EU law. It was originally associated with the directives. According to the Court of Justice: 'the Member States' obligation arising from a directive to achieve the result envisaged by the directive and their duty under article 5 of the Treaty to take all appropriate measures, whether general or particular, to ensure the fulfilment of that obligation, is binding on all the authorities of Member States including, for matters within their jurisdiction, the courts. It follows that, in applying the national law and in particular the provisions of a national law specifically introduced in order to implement directive [...], national courts are required to interpret their national law in the light of the wording and the purpose of the directive in order to achieve the result referred to in the third paragraph of article 189. [...] It is for the national court to interpret and apply the legislation adopted for the implementation of the directive in conformity with the requirements of community law, in so far as it is given discretion to do so under national law'.[31] The Court of Justice resolved here a question whether the directive may have some legal effects even though its provisions do not meet requirements laid down by *Van Gend en Loos* formula (are not sufficiently clear, precise and unconditional) and thus they cannot be directly applicable. It replied this question in the affirmative because it stated an obligation of national courts to interpret their law in line with the meaning of the directive. The arguments for the imposition of such a new duty on national authorities were based on the binding nature of directives and the principle of loyalty (article 4, paragraph 2, third subparagraph 3 TEU) which impose to Member States the duty to take any measures to fulfil the obligations conferred upon them by Treaties.

---

[30]Michal Bobek recalls these three options as weak, medium and strong indirect effect (Bobek 2014).

[31]Von Colson and Kamann vs. Land Nordrhein-Westfalen, 14/83, ECLI:EU:C:1984:153, points 27–28.

The subsequent case law of the Court of Justice brought the substantial development of the principle of the indirect effect. The duty to interpret national law in the light of EU norms evolved both qualitatively and quantitatively. At the very beginning it covered only the duty to interpret national law adopted in order to implement directives in the light of this particular directive. It was introduced as some kind of alternative to the lacking direct effect (Betlem 2002) but developed to the influential impact of EU regulative power. The crucial expansions were brought by the decision in *Marleasing*[32] case where Court of Justice brought a clarification of some problematic aspects of this principle:

- It extended the scope of national law that has to be interpreted in the light of rules of EU law. One of the most problematic issues of the doctrine of indirect effect was whether the duty of consistent interpretation covers only that part of the national law that implemented a certain directive into the national legal system of the Member State or whether it covers also other national laws whose adoption was not related with the implementation. The Court of Justice stated that duty of consistent interpretation has to be understood widely and acknowledged that indirect effect covers all the national law even that which was not adopted in the connection with the implementation of the directive and no matter whether it was adopted before or after the adoption of the directive. Basically the principle of indirect effect affects the national legal order as a whole (including the national constitutions).
- Another important issue is that Court of Justice acknowledged the impact of indirect effect also in so-called horizontal relationships. National courts are according to this wide view obliged to interpret the national law in a harmony with EU requirements even in disputes between individuals, where indirect effect served mainly as an alternative to the prohibition of horizontal direct effect of directives.

The indirect effect stands as a 'robust' EU law principle (Bobek 2014) and its wide consequences seem to be more crucial for the national sovereignty and national law autonomy discussions than the direct applicability and primacy. It is because indirect effect is connected with all provisions of EU law and touches all fields of national law and is capable to turn the established way of interpretation of domestic norms (and therefore the adjudication processes). However, this wide influence is balanced by the fact that it is still national law, which is applied here. In comparison with direct effect and primacy we do not face here the penetration of norms produced by different public power and replacement of national norms. It is also worth to say here, that direct effect is not limitless. Court of Justice expressed several boundaries of EU-consistent interpretation of national law, which more or less should act to protect its autonomy. It has formulated following rules in the connection with the limits of obligation of national judges to interpret the national law in the light of the European Union norms:

---

[32]Marleasing vs. Comercial Internacional de Alimentación, C-106/89, ECLI:EU:C:1990:395.

- The interpretation of the national law in the light of European Union law provisions is limited by the scope of discretionary competences of the national authority applying law and interpretation methods governed by the national law (*Von Colson*).
- The EU-consistent interpretation of the national law may not lead into conclusions denying the essence of the national legislation, i.e. to decisions *contra legem* (*Marleasing*).
- The position of an individual may not be aggravated in the meaning of the establishment or the extension of the criminal responsibility (*Kolpinghuis*[33]).
- In case of indirect effect of a directive the obligation of the harmonious interpretation may be established only after the expiration of the period prescribed for the implementation of a directive (*Adeneler*[34]).

2.4.3.3 The Price for the Non-conformity—State Liability for Damages Caused by Breaches of EU Law

The principle of state liability is usually perceived as remedy used to enforce the individual right prescribed by the EU law (Aalto 2011). This principle completes the aforementioned characteristics of the EU law as a complex and autonomous legal order. The liability for damages is certain subsidiary consequence which serves as a tool to protect individuals in case when State breaches its obligations deriving from its commitments as a Member of the EU. From another point of view, this remedy widens the notion of dominance of EU law and has a special relevance for the 'sovereignty discussions'. This special European remedy is an example of 'interventionist approach' (Dougan 2004) of the Court of Justice to the scale of national remedies. Its wide evolution in the Court's case law touches upon the autonomy of national (remedial) law but also interfere with the sensitive questions like sovereignty of national legislators and independence of national courts. This principle closes the circle of dominance by introduction of responsibility regime connected with 'ignorance' of EU law rules by the Member States.

The pilot decision forming this doctrine was issued in case *Francovich.*[35] Form and conditions were subsequently governed by following case law of the Court of Justice. The Court of Justice understands the liability of the Member States for damages as one of the key principles of EU law inherent to the system of the Treaty. According to the Court of Justice the liability is a matter of principle because: 'It should be borne in mind at the outset that the EEC Treaty has created its own legal system, which is integrated into the legal systems of the Member States and which their courts are bound to apply. The subjects of that legal system are not only the Member States but also their nationals. Just as it imposes burdens on individuals,

[33]Kolpinghuis Nijmegen, 80/86, ECLI:EU:C:1987:431.

[34]Adeneler and others, C-212/04, ECLI:EU:C:2006:443.

[35]Francovich and Bonifaci vs. Italy, C-6/90 and C-9/90, ECLI:EU:C:1991:428.

Community law is also intended to give rise to rights which become part of their legal patrimony. Those rights arise not only where they are expressly granted by the Treaty but also by virtue of obligations which the Treaty imposes in a clearly defined manner both on individuals and on the Member States and the Community institutions […]. Furthermore, it has been consistently held that the national courts whose task it is to apply the provisions of Community law in areas within their jurisdiction must ensure that those rules take full effect and must protect the rights which they confer on individuals […]. The full effectiveness of Community rules would be impaired and the protection of the rights which they grant would be weakened if individuals were unable to obtain redress when their rights are infringed by a breach of Community law for which a Member State can be held responsible'.[36] Court of Justice clearly recalled here to the notion of autonomy and effectiveness of EU law. It repeated also the loyalty commitment of the Member States. The style of the judgement and arguments used by the Court are very close to the constitutionally landmark decisions (*Costa, Van Gend, Simmenthal,* actually quoted by the Court) and puts this decision on the same level of importance.

Significant development and clarification of problematic issues related to the liability doctrine were brought by the Court of Justice in *Brasserie du Pêcheur* case.[37] One of the problems not covered by the *Francovich* case was the question whether the Member States are liable for damages also in cases where they breach the directly applicable rule of supranational law. The government of Member States argued against the rise of liability in this situation and reasoned their position by the plea that the direct effect is an adequate instrument to protect rights of individuals, that there are sufficient national instruments for claiming the reparation and thus it is not necessary to held the state responsible for the infringement also under the EU law. The Court of Justice refused this argument and stated that the direct effect is not a satisfactory instrument to ensure the effectivity of individuals' remedy for coverage of suffered harm. This principle entitles individuals to seek the EU law directly in the proceedings before the national court but it does not guarantee the reparation for damages and loss caused by the breach of State's obligations. The doctrine of the State's liability for damages complements the principle of the direct effect but it is an autonomous notion within the complex system of EU law. The judgment also contributed significantly to the development of conditions of the State liability for damages. Court did not formulate the precise definition of the liability but it lay down that the liability is conditional on many circumstances (such as a precise definition of discretionary competences of the state's authority, clarity or non-clarity of the infringed norms, etc.). According to this decision the liability conditions state as follows:

[36] Francovich and Bonifaci vs. Italy, C-6/90 and C-9/90, ECLI:EU:C:1991:428, points 31–35.

[37] Brasserie du Pêcheur vs. Bundesrepublik Deutschland and The Queen/Secretary of State for Transport, ex parte Factortame and others, C-46/93 and C-48/93, ECLI:EU:C:1996:79.

- the infringed rules of EU law shall prescribe or at least presume the existence of certain subjective rights of individual;
- there must be a direct causal link between the breach of EU law and the loss or damage caused;
- the breach of EU law caused by the State authorities must be sufficiently serious. The definition of the seriousness of the breach depends on the clarity of the Union rule infringed and further on the margin of a discretion left by the EU law to the national authority

  (1) In case of a narrow margin of discretion or no discretion, any infringement of the Member State obligation is sufficient to be described as the serious breach.
  (2) In case of a broad margin of a discretion of national authority it is further necessary to prove the seriousness by subsidiary arguments, for instance a fault, a conduct contrary to the settled case law, a contributory fault of an individual, a certain margin of Union co-liability deriving from the unclear definition of the state obligations, etc.

In *Brasserie du Pêcheur,* the Court of Justice also clarified the question for the conduct (or omission) of which national authorities the Member States should be responsible. Here it stated that the States are liable regardless whether the breach of EU law was caused by an authority representing legislative or executive power. Further the Court of Justice broadened the sum of national authorities for whose acts the State may be held responsible. The categories were widened to the local authorities (*Konle*[38]; *Haim*[39]) and also to the national judiciary (*Köbler*[40]*; Traghetti del Mediterraneo*[41]).

The liability of the State for the acting of the authorities representing the judicial power is one of the most sensitive issues of the EU law (because of the judicial independence, the wide discretion, etc.) and it is the subject to some additional conditions (Breuer 2004). According to the Court of Justice the Member State should be held responsible for the damage and loss caused by the breach of the European Union law only under the circumstances that this damage was caused by the decision of national court of the last instance and that infringement of the EU law rule by the national court was sufficiently manifest (arbitrary). However, Member States cannot pose any special limitations or conditions for the claims of individuals for compensation of damages caused by such manifest breach of EU law. For example, restriction of the liability of Member State for the activity of the judiciary only to the cases involving intentional fault or gross negligence of justices is incompatible with the general principle of the liability of Member States for a breach of EU law (*Commission v Italy*[42]).

---

[38]Konle, C-302/97, ECLI:EU:C:1999:271.

[39]Haim, C-424/97, ECLI:EU:C:2000:357.

[40]Köbler, C-224/01, ECLI:EU:C:2003:513.

[41]Traghetti del Mediterraneo, C-173/03, ECLI:EU:C:2006:391.

[42]Commission vs. Italy, C-379/10, ECLI:EU:C:2011:775.

2.5 'Cerberus' Guarding the Fundamental Rights[43]

Nowadays, the key provisions which define the Union as a constitutional community based on respect for human rights are included in the Treaty on European Union. The most important are article 2 TEU (which defines the values of European Union and presents the human rights as the fundamental core of the integration), article 6 TEU (which defines or summarizes the sources and several instruments of the human rights protection within the European Union) and article 7 (which introduces the mechanism of control and sanctioning of the Member States in the cases of grave violation of the fundamental rights by them).

The central provision is the second aforementioned provision (article 6 TEU) which defines the three cornerstones of the protection of fundamental rights at the supranational level. These three totems seems to provide Union within the most complex system of the promotion of fundamental rights which shall work as the one body of tools with three different heads—like the Cerberus guarding the mythic underworld.

Moreover, this strong impetus on the role of fundamental rights within the supranational legal order serves as an indirect tool of defence of supranational (Court's) view on the nature of the legal system of the Community and Union, respectively (Craig 2010). The recognition of fundamental rights as immanent part of supranational law and establishment of the complex system of their protection rendered to the supranational legal system the nature of the constitutional order. Therefore, it was suitable to be accepted by the national courts in their practice as the law applicable in their judicial decision-making. The big lesson here was learned in connection with the famous 'Solange saga' of German Federal Constitutional Court (Frowein 1988). German court primarily rejected the possibility of unlimited application of Community law within the national legal practice by the argument that supranational law showed serious deficiencies in the field of protection of individuals. It stated that as long as Community system will show the deficiencies (in comparison with German level) it will not accept its general internal effects (case *Solange I*[44]). Once the Community system improved and the doctrine of fundamental rights was introduced the Federal Constitutional Court changed its opinion and accepted the application of Community rules (case *Solange II*[45]) but once more with the objection that It will serve as the ultima ratio guardian of the structural quality of this reached level. In case when serious structural discrepancies will appear within the supranational system the German court reserves itself the right not to accept the internal applicability of the certain rules of EU law within

[43]This chapter is based on my previous work with title Idolatry of Rights and Freedoms—Reflections on the Autopoietic Role of Fundamental Rights within Constitutionalization of the European Union, which was published in volume Protecting Human Rights in the EU. Controversies and Challenges of the Charter of Fundamental Rights (see Hamuľák 2014).

[44]Solange I—Internationale Handelsgesellschaft von Einfuhr—und Vorratsstelle für Getreide und Futtermittel, decision of 29 May 1974, BVerfGE 37, 271.

[45]Solange II—Wünsche Handelsgesellschaft decision of 22 October 1986, BVerfGE 73, 339.

German system (Lebeck 2006). This raised finger is still valid (see its repetitions in *Maastricht-Urteil*[46] as well as in *Lissabon-Urteil*[47]) and transmitted also to the approach of other Member States courts (Czech Constitutional Court may serve as one of the most influenced examples, see cases *Sugar Quotas*[48]; *European Arrest Warrant,*[49] *Lisbon I*[50] and *Lisbon II*[51]). And within this atmosphere of permanent control from the national level the supranational approach to the protection of fundamental rights has to develop perpetually in nowadays and also in the future. Therefore, Union is bound by the sources and mechanisms and therefore it is still willing to go further—mainly by the accession to the European Convention.

2.5.1 Charter of Fundamental Rights of the European Union—Internal Pillar

Granting the legally binding force to the Charter of Fundamental Rights of the European Union (Charter) via adoption of Treaty of Lisbon (by reference included in the first paragraph of the article 6 TEU) brought significant changes within the EU legal system as whole. Charter was adopted in December 2000 as mere political declaration without legally binding nature. First attempt to make it legally binding came in connection with the Treaty establishing Constitution for Europe. Here, the Charter was included directly to the text of European Constitution. But because this reform document was rejected by the French and Dutch people in referendums in 2005 the question of the binding force of the Charter was not resolved yet. Second (successful) attempt was made in connection with the Treaty of Lisbon. This document changed the wording of article 6 TEU and introduced the 'legalisation' clause according to which Charter got the same legal value as the Treaties. Starting by 1st December, 2009 (when Treaty of Lisbon entered into the force) the Charter of fundamental rights of the European Union became legally binding (Forejtová 2013).

Thanks to the Charter the project of European integration entered a new stage and got a new image. Union obtained an internal instrument of identification and protection of human rights, which is the first pillar of the whole system. Breakthrough importance of adopting a legally binding catalogue of fundamental rights has several aspects:

- It can be viewed from the perspective of constitutional dogmatic where adoption of own internal catalogue of rights and freedoms completes the constitutional

[46]Maastricht-Urteil decision of 12 October 1993, BVerfGE 89, 155.

[47]Lissabon-Urteil decision of 30 June 2009, 2 BvE 2/08.

[48]Sugar Quotas III, Pl. ÚS 50/04, ECLI:CZ:US:2006:Pl.US.50.04.

[49]European Arrest Warrant, Pl. ÚS 66/04, ECLI:CZ:US:2006:Pl.US.66.04.

[50]Treaty of Lisbon I, Pl. ÚS 19/08, ECLI:CZ:US:2008:Pl.US.19.08.1.

[51]Treaty of Lisbon II, Pl. ÚS 29/09, ECLI:CZ:US:2009:Pl.US.29.09.3.

system of the Union. Next to the more or less established formal/procedural constitutional rules (relations of the Union and the Member States, the internal rules of separation of powers between a several Union institutions, quasi-federal rules on the application of Union law in the national practice, etc.) it brought clear material constitutional rules defining the relationship between the individual and public authorities into the to the supranational constitutional system.[52] Charter itself legitimizes the EU public power in 'black letter' understanding. Its active use as the source of legality review by the Court of Justice deepens this impact in real world (De Búrca 2013).[53]

- Moreover, this step can be evaluated from the perspective of some constitutional symbolism where the existence of the human rights catalogue serves as important legitimizing tool (Neacsu 2001) vis-á-vis ever-expanding and deepening powers of the European Union or Member States acting on behalf of Union. Lenaerts and Cambien speak about increasing of the output democracy of the EU in this regard. Charter legitimizes EU with the same value as increased role of principle of representation and parliamentarism in the EU (the input democracy) (Lenaerts and Cambien 2009).
- From another point of view Charter fulfilled the requirement of improvement of legal certainty of the holders of fundamental rights by making these rights visible and manifested. It confirmed the attitude of the Court of Justice towards the fundamental rights from the previous decades. But it is true that great deal made by the Court of Justice by introduction of the fundamental rights as General Principles (see further) was always connected with the risk of uncertainty and unpredictability. As AG Mazák rightly stressed in his Opinion in *Palacios* case: '[…] in the nature of general principles of law, which are to be sought rather in the Platonic heaven of law than in the law books, that both their existence and their substantive content are marked by uncertainty'.[54] Charter is the tool of minimalizing of that uncertainty and this seems to be its crucial added value.
- Additionally, the legally binding Charter serves as an important revolutionary novelty in terms of theory and history of human rights. Charter by its wide content revolutionizes the classic approach to human rights which used to be

[52]Contours of material constitutionality of the European Union are defined primarily by the system of protection of fundamental rights. The question of the role and place of fundamental rights within the European Communities and the European Union has undergone major developments during the history of integration (Šišková 2008). But it is non-disputable that only by adoption of the binding catalogue it reached the level of complexity and clarity.

[53]As very visible example of the real impact of the Charter one may recall to the crucial decision of the Court of Justice *Digital Rights Ireland*, C-293/12, ECLI:EU:C:2014:238, where Court used the Charter as the main argument for the (surprising) invalidation of the so-called Data Retention Directive (2002/58/EC) as whole. Another strong example is *Opinion on the Agreement on Accession of the European Union to the European Convention for the Protection of Human Rights and Fundamental Freedoms*, 2/13, ECLI:EU:C:2014:2454, where Court of Justice found the incompatibility between the proposed agreement and EU law including the Charter (stating the doubts about sufficient protection of autonomy of Charter, see points 186–190).

[54]AG Opinion, Félix Palacios de la Villa, C-411/05, ECLI:EU:C:2007:106.

recognized by the separate documents in line with the theory of several human rights generations. Charter abandons this traditional approach at least formally and recognizes the civil and political rights as well as economic, social and cultural rights as part of one general human rights record.
- Last but not least, the Charter reaches also the spheres of the Member States as they are included into the list of 'negative' addresses—the entities obliged to respect the Charter. We can see one more the federal impetus here. Charter as the catalogue of the 'centre' binds the several parts of the Union and attributes the one standard all over the entire community.

Charter is very complex and quite ambitious document. It includes the tens of human rights from all generations (classical division of human rights to the three generations of rights: civil and political; economic, social and cultural; the modern = solidarity rights). It has its own special structure which does not follow the classical division of human rights to types or generations. The 'body of Charter' includes 50 material and 4 horizontal provisions (+explanations which are attached to the catalogue). It is internally structured into the seven titles

- First title called 'dignity' (articles 1–5) is inspired by 'Kantian' ideal concepts, i.e. human dignity at the first place. It includes the hard core rights as rights to life, protection of personal integrity, prohibition of torture, etc.
- Second title entitled 'freedoms' (articles 6–19) deals with the various examples of personal liberties like personal freedom, protection of private spheres, freedom of thought and expression, freedom of association and assembly, etc.).
- Third title called 'equality' (articles 20–26) stresses the fact that anti-discrimination policy is one of the most important fields of activity of the Union. There is big variety of equality general anti-discrimination clause, equality between men and women, special protection of vulnerable groups—children, elderly and people with disabilities, etc.
- Fourth title marked 'solidarity' (articles 27–38) includes mainly the economic and social rights, e.g. collective bargaining and action, fair and just working conditions, access to health care, etc.
- Fifth title called 'Citizen's rights' (articles 39–46) is inspired by the Treaty provisions on Union's citizenship. It repeats the classical group of rights of Union's citizens (electorate rights, free movement, political rights and diplomatic protection) and adds quite detail provision on the righto good administration.
- Sixth title is identified as 'Justice' (articles 47–50) and includes the procedural safeguards as right to fair trial, presumption of innocence, legality and proportionality of criminal justice, *ne bis in idem* principle).
- Seventh title includes so-called horizontal provision which determines the general rules of application and interpretation of Charter and presents the sources of inspiration for the adoption of this document (articles 51–54).

Very important provision which has to be mentioned in this introductory elaboration of the Charter is article 51 paragraph 1. It defines the addresses of obligation to respect the rights included in the Charter. There are two categories of addresses which have obligation to respect of the Charter:

- Institutions, bodies, offices and agencies of the Union—here the Charter serve as the tool of strengthening of rule of law and democratic legitimacy of the supranational governance. It is the goal of long path on which Communities and Union were finding the ideal tool for the protection of fundamental rights. Institutions of the EU are responsible to respect rights protected by the Charter generally in all activities which could touch upon individuals' rights.
- Member States—here Charter brings the federalisation question on the scene. The question of existence of common (central) standard of fundamental rights protection binding upon all Member States (peripheries) is clearly interconnected with the above-mentioned emancipation and dominance of EU law. And it deepens the scope of protection of individuals within the whole system of application of EU law. But it is worth to mention here that not all Member States' conducts fall under Charter conformity test. It is clear from the wording of article 51 paragraph 1 that Charter is applicable vis-á-vis Member States 'only when they are implementing Union law'. The Charter (unlike for example the European Convention on Human Rights and Fundamental Freedoms) is not universally applicable. Its applicability occurs where the conduct of a Member State has some EU dimension. The question is not whether Member states must fulfil the Charter but to what extent they have to do that. By resolving this problem we will answer the question of intensity of federal impacts of the Charter itself. This important query is covered by the next section of this chapter.

The widening of effects of Charter to the conducts of Member States is not a novelty or systemic revolution in EU law. Even before the adoption of the Charter, the Court of Justice recognized the applicability of EU fundamental rights standards (as unwritten general principles of law) on the selected activities of Member States and recognized that national courts must follow these principles in their decisions. EU law recognized certain situations where Member States held the duty to respect supranational standards of fundamental rights protection:

(a) The basic form, i.e. the explicit situations where some EU legislation directly introduces a specific obligation to protect the fundamental right (typically in the area of anti-discrimination law or general duty to ensure judicial remedies to protect individual rights steaming from EU law, e.g. *Johnston*[55] or *Defrenne*[56] cases).
(b) The 'agent' situations, i.e. the situations where Member States were imple menting or applying a Union law. This so-called *Wachauf* situation[57] is

[55]Johnston vs. Chief Constable of the Royal Ulster Constabulary, 222/84, ECLI:EU:C:1986:206.

[56]Defrenne vs. SABENA, 43/75, ECLI:EU:C:1976:56.

[57]Wachauf, 5/88 ECLI:EU:C:1989:321. See also Bosphorus vs. Minister for Transport, Energy and Communications and Others, C-84/95, ECLI:EU:C:1996:312.

interconnected with phenomenon of decentralized governance when state authorities act essentially as an extended arm of the European Union. Weiler points out that in the background of this argument there is a need to use a single standard of European Union law in all states (Weiler 1999).

(c) And a derogation model, i.e. the cases where Member States (within their scope of discretion) derogate from the Internal Market rules (uses permitted exemptions from the prohibition of restrictions on freedom of movement). This so-called *ERT* situation[58] differs to both former types. Here Member States apply their own law and do not behave as implementers of EU decisions. But still even when applying their national law, they do so thanks to permission of the EU rules and for the purpose to deviate from EU rules. So they appear in the area outlined by EU law (Weiler 1999). The arguments here, similar to previous situations, are based on the general need for a uniform standard of the application of EU law in all states.

It is thus clear that the application of the Charter by the Member States is limited only to a certain segment of their activities somehow connected with the effects of EU law. The question is, what this segment covers, which actions of the Member States fall under the umbrella of the Charter (and therefore under control and interpretative jurisdiction of the Court of Justice)?

This question was among the most discussed issues in relation to the negotiation of the Charter (Schönlau 2005) and brought a significant case law of the Court of Justice in recent where Court of Justice upheld above-mentioned broad interpretation of article 51 paragraph 1 is the judgment in *Fransson* case.[59] In this case the Court of Justice answered a preliminary question from the Swedish court, which concerned criminal proceedings against H.Å. Fransson for serious tax evasion. H.Å. Fransson was charged for stating false information in tax returns and for failing to declare employers' contributions for the certain accounting periods. The problem was that two years before Swedish tax authorities ordered him to pay some tax surcharge for the same tax misconducts. National court therefore faced the problem whether previous administrative sanction and new criminal prosecution fall under prohibition of double jeopardy. And since the Charter confirms principle of *ne bis in idem* in article 50 it was confronted with the potential conflict of national rules with the EU human rights catalogue. Therefore, it decided to stay proceedings and turned to the Court of Justice with the preliminary question. The circumstances of the case opened the initial question whether tax penalties and related criminal proceedings represent the implementation of EU law within the meaning of article 51 paragraph 1 of the Charter? Part of the Member States[60] European Commission and the Advocate General (Cruz Villalón) reflected this question negatively and rejected the applicability of the Charter and therefore the Court's jurisdiction to decide the case.

---

[58]ERT, C-260/89, ECLI:EU:C:1991:254. See also Familiapress, C-368/95, ECLI:EU:C:1997:325.

[59]Åkerberg Fransson, C-617/10, ECLI:EU:C:2013:105.

[60]Sweden, Czech Republic, Denmark, Ireland and Netherlands.

However, the Court of Justice took the opposite view and recognized the applicability of the Charter despite the fact that it was neither a classic case of the implementation of EU law (*Wachauf* situation), nor the case of derogation from EU rules (*ERT* situation). It extended the scope of application of the Charter vis-á-vis Member States also to other (much more broad) situations. According the Court: 'Since the fundamental rights guaranteed by the Charter must therefore be complied with where national legislation falls within the scope of European Union law, situations cannot exist which are covered in that way by European Union law without those fundamental rights being applicable. The applicability of European Union law entails applicability of the fundamental rights guaranteed by the Charter'.[61] The wide understanding of the Court of Justice lies in fact that term 'applicability' in its view does not mean a concrete situation of application of EU rules in specific case, but basically just a sort of their factual abstract existence. It is not important whether EU law was used (directly or indirectly) in concrete case. The key feature for applicability of the Charter is that circumstance of the case falls within the scope of EU law. To meet this test even partial or indirect connection to Union law is sufficient (Hancox 2013). This requirement was met in the case of H.Å. Fransson. His tax offenses were partly related to the area of value added tax, which forms an area harmonized by EU law. Moreover, part of the revenue from VAT constitutes one of the own resources of the Union budget. According to the Court of Justice these facts were satisfactory enough to build a bridge between prosecution at the national level and EU law. The matter therefore dropped within the scope of application of Union law and criminal prosecution of tax evasion here was considered as the implementation of EU law within the meaning of article 51 paragraph 1 of the Charter. Judgment in *Fransson* case brought an extremely broad interpretation of the Charters' impact on the conduct of Member States. The Charter became a shadow of European Union law (Lenaerts and Gutiérrez-Fons 2014) and its applicability became somewhat unpredictable. It's not surprising that interpretation offered by the Court of Justice opened the discussion about the very sensitive questions related to the problem whether there is any autonomous space for Member States conduct which should be free of 'testing by the Charter' and what are the definitive frontiers of the scope of the Charter (Fontanelli 2014).

The subsequent case law of the Court of Justice partially corrected the excessive abstractness of *Fransson* ruling and confirmed that there are still some autonomous domains of the Member States. Court of Justice brought some light to the unclear *Fransson* findings and offered (a bit complicated but still applicable) criteria of testing whether there is some connection between national law applied in the case and EU law (Pirker 2014). In case *Siragusa* Court of Justice stated that: 'In order to determine whether national legislation involves the implementation of EU law for the purposes of article 51 of the Charter, some of the points to be determined are whether that legislation is intended to implement a provision of EU law; the nature of that legislation and whether it pursues objectives other than those covered by EU

[61] Åkerberg Fransson, C-617/10, ECLI:EU:C:2013:105, point 21.

law, even if it is capable of indirectly affecting EU law; and also whether there are specific rules of EU law on the matter or capable of affecting it […]'.[62] This point brought a certain explanation to the concept'acting within the scope EU law' given by the *Fransson* judgment. The applicability of the Charter still requires that certain matter falls within the scope of EU law. But to make this conclusion one needs to find a specific interconnection between national law (decision) and concrete provisions of EU law. The Court concluded that applicability of the Charter to the acts of Member States necessarily presupposes the existence of a certain degree of connection between the EU law and relevant national law measures that goes beyond the mere similarity of areas concerned or indirect impact of one area to another. As the Court stated in the *Hernández* case: 'the mere fact that a national measure comes within an area in which the European Union has powers cannot bring it within the scope of EU law, and, therefore, cannot render the Charter applicable […]'.[63]

From the case law (before and after Lisbon reform) follows a fairly wide range of understanding the concept of 'implementing' of EU law by Member States, which creates the potential for wide impact of the Charter on the national practice. But the important finding is that Charter cannot be used as the vehicle to widen the EU competences alone without any further relation to the existing scope of EU law. As the Court of Justice stated repeatedly[64] the Charter alone is not capable to establish its own competence. To sum up the notion of implementation of EU law covers both the direct application of EU rules and the application and interpretation of national rules that serves as transposition of EU sources, moreover, it regulates the application of national rules which could lead to derogation of EU-based entitlements (most in the internal market) and finally it covers the application/interpretation of national rules that relate to specific areas of Union competence settled by concrete EU law provisions.

2.5.2 European Convention for the Protection of Human Rights and Fundamental Freedoms—External Pillar

The second paragraph of article 6 TEU includes the commitment of the Union to accede to the European Convention for the Protection of Human Rights and Fundamental Freedoms (ECHR). This provision is a reflection of established

[62]Siragusa, C-206/13, ECLI:EU:C:2014:126, point 25.

[63]Julian Hernández and Others, C-198/13, ECLI:EU:C:2014:2055, point 36.

[64]Torralbo Marcos, ECLI:EU:C:2014:187, C-265/13, point 30; *Sociedade Agrícola e Imobiliária da Quinta de S. Paio,* C-258/13, EU:C:2013:810, point 20; *Dutka and Sajtos* C-614/12 and C-10/13, ECLI:EU:C:2014:30, point 15; *Weigl,* C-332/13, ECLI:EU:C:2014:31, point 14; *Cholakova*, C-14/13, ECLI:EU:C:2013:374, point 30; *Nagy and Others*, C-488/12, ECLI:EU:C:2013:703, point 17.

practice, when the Court of Justice in its case law[65] commonly refers to the ECHR as the source of its inspiration (Douglas-Scott 2006).

Even though accession negotiations had been commenced right at the beginning of 2010 and after intensive work (Králová 2011) they led to the final proposal of the Agreement on the Accession of the European Union to the Convention in April 2013 (Gragl 2013) EU still is not a party to the ECHR. The draft Agreement on Accession was evaluated by the Court of Justice according to article 218 paragraph 11 TFEU and this procedure led to the well-known negative *Opinion 2/13*[66] from 18th December 2014. In this opinion, Court of Justice refused the draft of the agreement for its incompatibility with the EU law. The Court gave uncompromising opinion according to which: 'The agreement on the accession of the European Union to the European Convention for the Protection of Human Rights and Fundamental Freedoms is not compatible with Article 6(2) TEU or with Protocol (No 8) relating to Article 6(2) of the Treaty on European Union on the accession of the Union to the European Convention on the Protection of Human Rights and Fundamental Freedoms'. The main reasons for this negative opinion were the risk for the autonomous character of the EU law, risk to the mutual trust between Member States, insufficient reflection of the specifics of the Common foreign and security policy of the EU and deficit in preservation of the special position of the Court of Justice by the efficient prior involvement mechanism. The Opinion of the Court was evaluated and criticized from many angles. It is not the aim of this volume to analyse the opinion and therefore I just refer to the significant literature on the topic.[67]

Actually, we are facing the deadlock situation in the accession process. Notwithstanding that, the accession is still the vivid matter as it was introduced as the constitutional duty of the Union by the adamant formulation in the article 6 paragraph 2 TEU (Grabenwarter and Pabel 2013). The accession is important goal of the Union but it is to some extent rather a symbolic act. By the accession to the ECHR Union will show the determination and readiness to be subject to the same control mechanism as its Member (and other European) countries. It is clear even from the statement of the Committee preparing the accession which says that 'As a result of the accession, the acts, measures and omissions of the EU, like every other High Contracting Party, will be subject to the external control exercised by the Court in the light of the rights guaranteed under the Convention. This is all the more important since the EU member States have transferred substantial powers to the EU'.[68] On the other hand, it is worth to say, that importance of ECHR as the external pillar of

[65]Nold v Commission, 4/73, ECLI: EU:C:1974:51; Rutili vs. Ministre de l'intérieur, 36/75, ECLI: EU:C:1975:137; Hauer vs. Land Rheinland-Pfalz 44/79, ECLI:EU:C:1979:290; *ERT*, C-260/89, ECLI: EU:C:1991:254; Kadi and Al Barakaat International Foundation v Council and Commission, C-402/05 P and C-415/05 P, ECLI: EU:C:2008:461 etc.

[66]Opinion on the Agreement on Accession of the European Union to the European Convention for the Protection of Human Rights and Fundamental Freedoms, 2/13, ECLI:EU:C:2014:2454.

[67]De Witte and Imamovic (2015); Nanopoulos (2015), Spaventa (2015) and many others.

[68]cParagraph 5 of the DRAFT Explanatory report to the Agreement on the Accession of the European Union to the Convention for the Protection of Human Rights and Fundamental Freedoms.

human rights protection in the EU will be preserved even without the accession. Above I wrote about stabile position of the ECHR as the source of inspiration for the Court of Justice when deciding the fundamental rights cases. This role of ECHR was underlined also in the third paragraph of the article 6 TEU[69] which referrers to this international treaty as one of the sources of the fundamental rights as the general principles of EU law. This provision drags the ECHR indirectly to the system of EU law even without formal accession. The importance of the ECHR is emphasized also by the article 52 paragraph 3[70] of the EU Charter of Fundamental Rights. This provision known as the *de minimise clause* preserves the reached level of protection of fundamental rights and introduces the hierarchy of a kind between Charter and ECHR. Finally, the action of the Union could be reviewed by the European Court for Human Rights indirectly via 'prosecuting' the Member States acting as the EU agents. According to the *Bospohus*[71] decision of European Court for Human Rights the complaints against Member States for the actions determined by the EU are acceptable if there is a lack of equivalent protection by the Union in comparison to the level of protection guaranteed by the ECHR. Taking into account all above-mentioned reflections of the ECHR it is right to conclude that EU has the external pillar of protection of fundamental rights—the European Convention for Protection of Human Rights and Fundamental Freedoms—even without building of formal bonds to this document.

2.5.3 Unwritten General Principles—Eternal Pillar

The third paragraph of article 6 TEU then identifies the last (but historically oldest) pillar of human rights protection on supranational level—the unwritten rules contained in the general principles of law. Even Union has it written catalogue (Charter) now, the importance of general principles is still high. First of all even when the Fathers of the treaty decided to state down explicitly the list of protected rights there is always a risk of deficiencies and incompleteness. There is also the phenomenon which may be determined by the phrase 'society overtake the law' which means that legal regulation is always somehow behind the evolutional

---

[69]Article 6 paragraph 3 TEU states: 'Fundamental rights, as guaranteed by the European Convention for the Protection of Human Rights and Fundamental Freedoms and as they result from the constitutional traditions common to the Member States, shall constitute general principles of the Union's law'.

[70]Article 52 paragraph 3 of the Charter states: 'In so far as this Charter contains rights which correspond to rights guaranteed by the Convention for the Protection of Human Rights and Fundamental Freedoms, the meaning and scope of those rights shall be the same as those laid down by the said Convention. This provision shall not prevent Union law providing more extensive protection'.

[71]Judgement of the European Court for Human Rights (Grand Chamber) of 30 June 2005, *Bosphorus Hava Yolları Turizm ve Ticaret Anonim Şirketi v. Ireland*, Application no. 45036/98.

features in technology and society which bring the new unknown problems. And the open category—as the principles are—is the best instrument for the flexible reaction and protection of individuals' rights in these circumstances. The development of the doctrine of fundamental rights as part of the general principles of law played a crucial role in building of the constitutionality of supranational entities.

Contours of material constitutionality of the European Union (remember that our third claim is 'where a rule of law is secured there is a constitution') are defined primarily by the system of protection of fundamental rights. The question of the role and place of fundamental rights within the European Communities and the European Union has undergone major developments during the history of integration.

The original text of founding documents did not pay any attention to this issue. Also the Court of Justice was originally very strict and by using of precise formal approach rejected the possibility of protection of fundamental rights within the Community legal system. The Court of Justice believed that then sources of Community law contained no (nor explicit nor implicit) basis for the protection of fundamental rights (see *Geitling* case[72]). The most quoted reasons for this initial resistance where:

- the dominant focus on the economic integration,
- the existence of the Council of Europe (another European organization which was established primarily for the protection and promotion of democracy, rule of law and fundamental freedoms),
- fundamental rights as a traditional domain of national constitutional law,
- absence of legal competence of the Community in the field of fundamental rights.

The silence of the Treaties and reluctance of the Court of Justice to possibility of fundamental rights protection had a negative impact in several aspects. It led to the reduction in quality of protection of individuals, tension between Community law and national law and decrease of legitimacy and democratic nature of European Communities. Therefore, this undesirable situation (with its negative consequences) was not sustainable for the long time. And it was the Court of Justice who brought the revolution and caused the end of 'dark era' in the approach to the fundamental rights.

In the seminal *Stauder*[73] Court of Justice turned its approach from strictly formal and positive to the material and stated that fundamental rights form the part of general principles of law on which the Community id based and prescribed itself the assignment to be their guardian. Court's doctrine of fundamental rights as part of the general principles of law laid the foundations of inner (supranational) prism to human rights protection. The importance of *Stauder* ruling is that Court of Justice

[72]Präsident Ruhrkohlen-Verkaufsgesellschaft and others vs. ECSC High Authority, 36/59, ECLI:EU:C:1960:36.

[73]Stauder vs. Stadt Ulm, 29/69, ECLI:EU:C:1969:57.

found the way how to safeguard the rule of law in cases of alleged violation of fundamental rights by actions of Community authorities. The court denied its own initial assertion that Community law does not contain any (no explicit nor implicit) rules providing for protection of fundamental rights.

In the next period of the evolution of this doctrine, the Court of Justice primarily pointed out particular sources of inspiration[74] which filled and precise the unspecified category of general principles of law. These sources of inspirations were constitutional traditions common to the Member States[75] and international treaties on human rights on which the Member States participate or are their signatories and in particular the European Convention for the Protection of Human Rights and Fundamental Freedoms.[76]

Fundamental rights encoded in the unwritten general principles of law become the only source of protection for long decades of existence of supranational entities. Recognition of human rights was important not only in terms of individuals and their protection. As I mentioned above, the doctrine of fundamental rights as a general principles served also as certain self-reference, the autonomous claim for the constitutionality of European integration entities which supported their accountability and legitimacy of their actions.

2.5.4 Autopoietic Role of Fundamental Rights

The recognition of human rights and the introduction of a system that monitors their observance are not important only for individual citizens and their protection as some universal pan-european superstructure (Klíma 2011). The doctrine of the general legal principles, the adoption of its own catalogue of human rights, and the will to surrender to an external (Strasbourg based) control mechanism, represent certain autopoiesis of the EU's constitutionalism (Torres Pérez 2009). It is clear that a constitution without fundamental rights is not a constitution (Holländer 2009). Only the recognition of the possibility to protect fundamental rights, only their

[74]It is important to stress the notion of "inspiration" here. Even though the Court of Justice was and still is open to draw inspiration from the national constitutional traditions and international sources it does not mean that all acknowledged rights are transposed to the supranational level automatically. Court of Justice understands the fundamental rights autonomously as the original part of supranational legal order and also offers an autonomous interpretation of the content of the fundamental rights. We may call it a "Community/Union view" with regard to the objectives of the Community/Union, which in some way limits the scope of protection afforded to fundamental rights (see Nold, 4/73, ECLI:EU:C:1974:51 or Hauer vs. Land Rheinland-Pfalz 44/79, ECLI:EU:C:1979:290, where fundamental right to property was to some extent suppressed by the Community economic and market interests).

[75]Internationale Handelsgesellschaft, 11/70, ECLI:EU:C:1970:114; Nold, 4/73, ECLI:EU:C:1974:51.

[76]Rutili vs. Ministre de l'intérieur, 36/75, ECLI:EU:C:1975:137; Hauer vs. Land Rheinland-Pfalz 44/79, ECLI:EU:C:1979:290.

recognition as an immanent component of the supranational legal system, gave this system the nature of a legal system. First and foremost, the case law of the Court of Justice and the subsequent adoption of the EU Charter of Fundamental Rights drew human rights into the system of EU law and they became the criterion of EU institutions' legitimacy.[77]

The introduction of human rights protection also serves as a strong unification tool, because shared values bond the European integration project (Dutheil de la Rochère and Pernice 2003). The failure to test the conformity of supranational law with fundamental individual rights would result in low legitimacy of this legal system and could jeopardize its emancipation and domination. Historical development confirms this because actual and potential human-legal deficits of the European Communities became key arguments against the obligation to accept supremacy of supranational law over national law. Standard-bearer of this approach was the German Federal Constitutional Court (Kirchhof 1999), which in a doctrine formed by its decisions in the so-called '*Solange* saga'[78] referred to the human-legal deficit of the Communities and its position became a catalyst for progress in this area on the supranational level. The Court's support of general legal principles not only resolved the human rights' protection deficit, but its doctrine served also as an indirect defence of its view regarding the nature of the EU legal system.

References

Aalto, P. (2011). *Public liability in EU law. Brasserie, Bergaderm and beyond*. Oxford: Hart Publishing.

Agnew, J. (2009). *Globalization and sovereignty*. Lanham: Rowman & Littlefield Publishers.

Alter, K. (2001). *Establishing the supremacy of European law*. New York: Oxford University Press.

Avbelj, M. (2011). Supremacy or primacy of EU law—(Why) does it matter? *European Law Journal, 17*(6), 744–763.

Avbelj, M., & Komárek, J. (Eds.). (2012). *Constitutional pluralism in the European union and beyond*. Oxford: Hart Publishing.

Bárány, E. (2007). *Pojmy dobrého práva [The notion of goof law]*. Bratislava: Eurokódex.

Barents, R. (2004). *The autonomy of community law*. Hague: Kluwer Law International.

Betlem, G. (2002). The doctrine of consistent interpretation—Managing legal uncertainty. *Oxford Journal of Legal Studies, 22*(3), 397–418.

Bobek, M. (2014). The effects of EU law in the national legal systems. In C. Barnard & S. Peers (Eds.), *European union law* (pp. 140–173). Oxford: Oxford University Press.

[77]For examples of ECJ judgements where it established a conflict between community acts with fundamental rights, see Oyowe and Traore v. Commission, 100/88, ECLI:EU:C:1989:638 or Prais v. Council, 130/75, ECLI:EU:C:1976:142.

[78]Federal Constitutional Court judgement of 29 May 1974, BVerfGE 37, 271 (Solange I) Internationale Handelsgesellschaft mbH. v. Einfuhr—und Vorratstelle für Getreide und Futtermittel and Federal Constitutional Court judgement of 22 October 1986, BVerfGE 73, 339 (Solange II) Re Wünsche Handelsgesellschaft.

Bobek, M., Bříza, P., & Komárek, J. (2011). *Vnitrostátní aplikace práva Evropské unie [Domestic application of EU law]*. Praha: C. H. Beck.
Breuer, M. (2004). State liability for judicial wrongs and community law: The case of Gerhard Köbler v. Austria. *European Law Review, 29*(1), 243–254.
Corrias, L. (2011). *The passivity of law. Competence and constitution in the European court of justice*. Dordrecht: Springer.
Craig, P. (1999). The nature of the community: Integration, democracy and legitimacy. In P. Craig & G. De Búrca (Eds.), *The evolution of EU law* (pp. 1–54). New York: Oxford University Press.
Craig, P. (2010). *The lisbon treaty. Law, politics and treaty reform*. New York: Oxford University Press.
Craig, P., & De Búrca, G. (2011). *EU law—Text, cases and materials* (5th ed.). Oxford: Oxford University Press.
De Búrca, G. (2013). After the EU charter of fundamental rights: The court of justice as a human rights adjudicator? *Maastricht Journal of European and Comparative Law, 20*(2), 168–184.
De Búrca, G., & Weiler, J. H. H. (Eds.). (2012). *The worlds of European constitucionalism*. New York: Cambridge University Press.
De Witte, B., & Imamović, Š. (2015). Opinion 2/13 on accession to the ECHR: Defending the EU legal order against a foreign human rights court. *European Law Review, 40*(5), 683–705.
Dougan, M. (2004). *National remedies before the Court of Justice*. Oxford: Hart Publishing.
Douglas-Scott, S. (2006). A tale of two courts: Luxembourg, strasbourg and the growing European human rights acquis. *Common Market Law Review, 43*(3), 629–665.
Dutheil de la Rochère, J., & Pernice, I. (2003). European Union law and national constitutions. In M. Andenas & J. Usher (Eds.), *The treaty of nice and beyond. Enlargement and constitutional reform* (pp. 47–105). Oxford: Hart Publishing.
Fontanelli, F. (2014). Implementation of EU Law through domestic measures after Fransson: The Court of Justice Buys Time and "non-preclusion" Troubles Loom Large. *European Law Review, 39*(5), 782–800.
Forejtová, M. (2011). Evropská unie jako subjekt mezinárodního práva veřejného [The European Union as a subject of international law]. In *Evropské právo [European Law]*. Plzeň: Aleš Čeněk.
Forejtová, M. (2013). *Diskriminace jako referenční kritérium v judikatuře evropských soudů [Discrimination as a reference in the case law of the European courts]*. Plzeň: Aleš Čeněk.
Forejtová, M. (2014). Občanství v judikatuře Soudního dvora Evropské unie v Evropském roce aktivního občanství [Citizenship by the Court of Justice of the European Union, the European Year of Active Citizenship]. *Acta Universitatis Carolinae - Iuridica, 60*(2), 45–55.
Forejtová, M. (2015). Recognition and enforcement of judgements within the EU—Or is it really so easy to achieve them? *The Lawyer Quarterly, 5*(1), 59–72.
Forejtová, M., & Tronečková, M. (2011). *Evropské právo v praxi [European law in practice]*. Plzeň: Aleš Čeněk.
Frowein, J. (1988). Solange II, (BVerfGE 73, 339) constitutional complaint Firma W. *Common Market Law Review, 25*(1), 201–206.
Grabenwarter, Ch., & Pabel, K. (2013). Commentary on article 6 TEU. In H.-J. Blanke & S. Mamgiameli (Eds.), *The treaty on European union. A commentary* (pp. 287–348). Heidelberg: Springer.
Gragl, P. (2013). *The accession of the European Union to the European Convention on human rights*. Oxford: Hart Publishing.
Habermas, J. (2001). *The postnational constellation. Political essays*. (M. Pensky, trans.). Cambridge, Massachusetts: The MIT Press.
Hamuľák, O. (2014). Idolatry of rights and freedoms—Reflections on the autopoietic role of fundamental rights within constitutionalization of the European Union. In T. Kerikmäe (Ed.), *Protecting human rights in the EU. Controversies and challenges of the charter of fundamental rights* (pp. 187–198). Berlin, Heidelberg: Springer.
Hancox, E. (2013). The meaning of "implementing" EU law under Article 51(1) of the charter: Åkerberg Fransson. *Common Market Law Review, 50*(5), 1411–1431.

Hinarejos, A. (2008). On the legal effects of framework decisions and decisions: Directly applicable, directly effective, self-executing, supreme? *European Law Journal, 14*(5), 620–634.

Holländer, P. (2009). *Základy všeobecné státovědy [The essentials of the general theory of state].* Plzeň: Aleš Čeněk.

Jacobs, F. G. (2007). *The sovereignty of law: The European way*. Cambridge: Cambridge University Press.

Jakab, A. (2006). Neutralizing the sovereignty question; compromise strategies in constitutional argumentations before European integration and since. *European Constitutional Law Review, 2*(3), 375–397.

Kelsen, H. (1944). The principle of sovereign equality of states as a basis for international organization. *The Yale Law Journal, 53*(2), 207–220.

Kiiver, P. (2012). *The early warning system for the principle of subsidiarity*. New York: Routledge.

Kirchhof, P. (1999). The balance of powers between national and european institutions. *European Law Journal, 5*(3), 225–242.

Klokočka, V. (2006). *Ústavní systémy evropských států [Constitutional systems of the European states]*. Praha: Linde.

Komárek, J. (2014). *Why national constitutional courts should not embrace EU fundamental rights*. London School of Economics. https://www.lse.ac.uk/collections/law/wps/WPS2014–23_Komarek.pdf. Accessed May 20, 2016.

Králová, J. (2011). Comments on the draft agreement on the accession of the European union to the convention for the protection of human rights and fundamental freedoms. *Czech Yearbook of Public & Private International Law, 2*(1), 127–142.

Lebeck, C. (2006). National constitutionalism, openness to international law and pragmatic limits of European integration—European Law in the German Constitutional Court from the EEC to PJCC. *German Law Journal, 7*(11), 907–945.

Leczykiewicz, D. (2009). *Constitutionalising the third pillar*. Centre for European Legal Studies. http://www.cels.law.cam.ac.uk/events/Leczykiewicz.pdf. Accessed November 21, 2015.

Lenaerts, K., & Cambien, N. (2009). The democratic legitimacy of the EU after the treaty of lisbon. In J. Wouters (Ed.), *European constitutionalism beyond Lisbon* (pp. 185–207). Antverps: Intersentia.

Lenaerts, K., & Gutiérrez-Fons, J. A. (2014). The place of the charter in the EU constitutional edifice. In S. Peers & T. Hervey, T. (Eds.), *The EU charter of fundamental rights. A commentary* (pp. 1600–1637). Oxford: Hart Publishing.

Lenaerts, K., & Van Nuffel, P. (2005). *Constitutional law of the European Union*. London: Sweet & Maxwell.

Lenaerts, K., & Van Nuffel, P. (2011). *European Union Law* (3rd ed.). London: Sweet and Maxwell.

Mac Amhlaigh, C. (2011). The European Union's constitutional mosaic: Big 'C' or small 'c', Is that a question? In N. Walker, J. Shaw, & S. Tierney (Eds.), *Europe's constitutional mosaic* (pp. 21–47). Oxford: Hart Publishing.

MacCormick, N. (1999). *Questioning sovereignty. Law, state, and nation in the European Commonwealth.* New York: Oxford University Press.

Mazák, J. (2011). Locus standi v konaní o neplatnosť: od Plaumannovho testu k regulačným aktom [Locus Standi in the legality review—From the Plaumann test towards regulatory acts), *Právník, 150*(3), 209–231.

Nanopoulos, E. (2015). Killing two birds with one stone? The Court of Justice's Opinion on the EU's Accession to the ECHR. *The Cambridge Law Journal, 74*(2), 185–188.

Neacsu, E. D. (2001). The Draft of the EU charter of fundamental rights: A step in the process of legitimizing EU as a political entity, and economic-social rights as fundamental human rights. *Columbia Journal of European Law, 1*(1), 141–146.

Niedobitek, M. (2009). Přednost práva EU a Lisabonská smlouva [Primacy of EU law and the treaty of Lisbon]. *Jurisprudence, 18*(1), 12–17.

Panke, D. (2010). *The effectiveness of the European Court of Justice. Why reluctant states comply* (329 p). Manchester: Manchester University Press.

Piris, J.-C. (2010). *The Lisbon Treaty. A legal and political analysis*. Cambridge: Cambridge University Press.

Pirker, B. (2014). Case C-206/13 Siragusa: A Further Piece for the Åkerberg Fransson Jigsaw Puzzle. European law blog http://europeanlawblog.eu/?p=2253. Accessed May 14, 2016.

Prechal, S. (2007). Direct effect, indirect effect, supremacy and the evolving constitution of the European Union. In C. Barnard (Ed.), *The fundamentals of EU Law revisited. Assessing the impact of the constitutional debate* (pp. 35–69). Oxford: Oxford University Press.

Přibáň, J. (2010). Multiple sovereignty: On Europe's self-constitutionalization and legal self-reference. *Ratio Juris, 23*(1), 41–64.

Schönlau, J. (2005). *Drafting the EU Charter—Rights, legitimacy and process*. London: Palgrave Macmillan.

Schütze, R. (2014). Constitutionalism and the European Union. In C. Barnard & S. Peers (Eds.), *European Union law* (pp. 71–96). Oxford: Oxford University Press.

Sehnálek, D. (2009). Effet utille a jeho projevy při interpretaci komunitárního práva [Effet utile and its expressions within the implementation of community law]. *Právník, 148*(8), 785–808.

Šišková, N. (2008). *The process of constitutionalisation of the EU and related issues*. Groningen: Europa Law Publishing.

Spaventa, E. (2015). A very fearful court? The protection of fundamental rights in the European Union after opinion 2/13. *Maastricht Journal of European and Comparative Law., 22*(1), 35–56.

Stein, E. (1981). Lawyers, judges, and the making of a transnational constitution. *The American Journal of International Law, 75*(1), 1–27.

Stein, E. (2005). The magic of the C-Word. *EUSA Review, 18*(3), 1–5.

Torres Pérez, A. (2009). *Conflict of rights in the European Union. A theory of supranational adjudication*. New York: Oxford University Press.

Weatherill, S. (2010). *Cases and materials on EU Law*. Oxford: Oxford University Press.

Weiler, J. H. H. (1991). The transformation of Europe. *The Yale Law Journal, 100*(8), 2401–2483.

Weiler, J. H. H. (1999). *The constitution of Europe. 'Do the new clothes have an Emperor?' and other essays on European integration*. New York: Cambridge University Press.

Wintr, J. (2004). Právně-politická metoda evropské integrace a návrh evropské ústavy [Legal and political method of European integration and proposal of constitution for Europe]. *České právo na prahu Evropské unie* (pp. 31–43). Karolinum: Praha.

Witte, B. (1999). The past and future of the European court of justice in the protection of human rights. In P. Alston (Ed.), *The EU and human rights* (pp. 859–897). Oxford: Oxford University Press.

Chapter 3
Shared Entitlement to Legitimate Violence in the EU and Its Theoretical Outcomes

3.1 Heterarchy of Sovereigns

First of all, we must admit that there is no specific autonomous original *pouvoir constituant* behind the processes of European integration. The EU does not have its own demos to serve as the source of constitutional power. There has been no constitutional revolution and the Member States were not united in some federal union by a single constitutional text. Member States are always present as building blocks of the EU and, despite the pressures of integration, they have not been swallowed by it. As the German Federal Constitutional Court clearly emphasized in its important Lisbon judgement[1] the 'state is not a myth' but is a fundamental form of the organization of the western society.

The Member States are the original holders of competences and remain independent units. Their right to withdraw from the Union, confirmed by the Treaty of Lisbon (see article 50 TEU) underlines this fact. Member States must be understood as the 'holders of their own destiny', the masters in case analogical to the Schmittian extreme situation. Carl Schmitt commences his Political Theology by the famous sentence 'sovereign is he who decides on the exception'. According to Schmitt the exception 'can at best be characterized as a case of extreme peril, a danger to the existence of the state, or the like' (Schmitt 1985). Even though in case of withdrawal we are not dealing with the danger to the sole existence of the state, the question whether to be or not to be a Member State is extreme enough for the transmission of this concept into the reflections on the role of state within the European integration.

On the other hand, the EU undoubtedly profiles itself as an independent entity, as some kind of sovereign which independently and individually manages the agenda entrusted to it by a transfer of competences from Member States. The EU is

[1] Lisbon judgement of Federal constitutional court of 30 June, 2009, 2 BvE 2/08, Absatz-Nr. 1/421. Available at http://www.bverfg.de/entscheidungen/es20090630 2bve000208en.html. For comments on this judgement, see i.e. Schorkopf (2009).

O. Hamuľák, *National Sovereignty in the European Union*,
SpringerBriefs in Law, DOI 10.1007/978-3-319-45351-4_3

a specific complex organism which disposes of independent decision-making tools and its own power mechanisms. It can autonomously and directly affect the legal status of legal subjects, and that makes it a form of public power, a self-governing subject, and a sovereign of its kind, which coexists with its basic units. We should mainly perceive EU sovereignty materially. It is obvious that, when talking about the EU's sovereignty (Večeřa 2001), we must consider the sum of the objectives that it should secure through its competences (Pavlíček et al. 2011). Sovereignty as an ability to meet specific regulatory functions autonomously can be assigned to a supranational entity. To reject such forms of sovereignty would mean the rejection of the fact that the EU can fulfil external[2] and internal tasks for which it holds responsibility. According to a former Judge of the German Federal Constitutional Court, Dieter Grimm, nation states no longer possess a monopoly on legal violence. Plenty of matters of high political importance are no longer decided by national institutions, governments and parliaments, but are determined in Brussels (Grimm and Bydžovská 2010). Partial transfer of the execution of legitimate violence would be hardly imaginable if not conducted by a sovereign entity.

Sovereignty of the EU is a product of blending functions, competences, but also unquantifiable factors, integration goals and some will to create a united Europe. Even CCC notes that: 'The core of European civilization includes values shared by all advanced world civilizations. These values are human liberty and human dignity, which form the basis of the self-determination of a human being. Functional forms of social cohabitation build on conscious self-limitation of an individual and on acceptance of order. The same principles lead to higher forms of effective human organization, whether it is a settlement, state or various forms of states' integration'.[3] I do not want, and cannot prove any 'mythical foundation' of European integration and sovereignty of integrating entities. In this respect, we often hear of the emergence of 'mythical' terminology in the early days of integration, when terms like 'founding fathers' and 'spirit of Treaties' were commonplaces (Cruz 2011). I neither seek an absolute sovereign or European Demos. I perceive EU sovereignty as a fact. The EU is a specific complex organism, which disposes of independent decision-making tools and own power mechanisms. It can autonomously and directly affect the legal status of legal subjects, and that makes it a form of public power, a self-governing subject, and a sovereign of its kind.

The development of the EU, its position and relationship with Member States, and above all the nature of its power tools (legal and political) make me define this entity as an autonomous subject based on its Member States' tolerance. That constitutional presentation of European supranational entities is tolerated or rather quietly accepted proves the fact that in key cases (*Costa*, *Simmenthal*, *Internationale Handelsgesellschaft*), the Member States only sporadically used

---

[2]When executing its external competences, the EU (or, respectively, its predecessor, the Community) has for quite some time been considered an autonomous subject of international law, which creates space for its comparison with a sovereign state (Meunier and McNamara 2007).

[3]Treaty of Lisbon I, Pl. ÚS 19/08, ECLI:CZ:US:2008:Pl.US.19.08.1, point 103.

their right to enter the proceedings in front of the Court (article 40 of the Statute of the Court of Justice of the European Union), despite the constitutional dimension of some of the issues (Stein 1981). The EU as a new sovereign assumes part of the political power traditionally assigned to the states. This phenomenon comes under the theory of global constitutionalism. The power of governance used to be generally related to national sovereignty, but today is transferred to other organizations and structures of a supranational or transnational system of politics and law. Therefore in connection with the EU, we may talk not only about divided or shared sovereignty but can even call it multiple sovereignty (Přibáň 2013). The political system and processes of governance within the EU entrust two types of subjects with similar duty—to accomplish the goals of integration (Brinkhorst 2009 or Stein 1999) speaks in this respect about a 'divided power system'. This type of system gives rise to a multilevel structure of 'mutually relatively independent [...] public powers' (Bárány 2009). Recognizing the EU's autonomy and accepting its independent constitutional processes while preserving the autonomy of its Member States brings, however, some complications. The system of European integration based on the plurality and separation of the actors creates a breeding ground for tension (MacCormick 1999) between EU law and national law of its Member States. This tension is based on diverse understandings of the legal basis of the EU legal system, on a distinct approach to grounds of its applicability (Borowski 2008). The Court of Justice considers EU law autonomous because it arises from its own source, i.e. the Treaties. National (constitutional) courts see the national applicability of EU law as being embodied in national constitutions (Maduro 1998). European Communities originally stood as a tabula rasa in terms of some constitutional culture (all the competences, functions and identity of European Communities were transferred from Member States). But as Walker reminds us, we must distinguish between this original state and the later situation when, due to the evolution of integration, elements of an own, autonomous constitutional culture emerged in the Community/Union (Walker 2006).

The relationship between supranational and national law undeniably implies a clash, the solution of which depends on the preferred point of view. Member States obviously favour the traditional perspective, and thus national law is perceived as a foundation which gives rise to international commitments of the state and is therefore paramount to EU norms. The opposite view is based on the argument of the emancipation of the EU law and promulgates the necessity for the effective and unified application of supranational norms. This inevitably requires their priority over national law.

In this binary world of two perspectives, we have to face a dilemma akin to two roosters in a hen house. The described war of legal systems (and their courts) cannot have a final winner, because there is no independent arbitrator with the authority to resolve conflicts between the EU and national law. Under these circumstances, only individual battles have winners and no one can win the war. The 'winner' is the court, which has the privilege to be the last to decide on each concrete case. The emergence of a new case gives the concerned actors an opportunity to argue for or against previous rulings made by the other side. And thus the circle may again be opened. An example of such conflict may be seen in the different approach of the Court of Justice and CCC to the evaluation of the so-called Slovak Pensions case. In the past, the CCC repeatedly stood up for the claims of Czech citizens—who were employed by an employer based in the Slovak part of the former federation—to receive compensation payment up to the level of their hypothetical pension, which they would have been entitled to had they worked in the Czech part of the common state. The Court of Justice *Landtová* judgement[4] ruled that the aforementioned special compensation was in breach of EU law on free movement and principles of non-discrimination on the basis of nationality (Forejtová 2013). This was because the pensions were being awarded solely to Czech nationals with permanent residence in the Czech Republic. In January 2012, CCC gave its verdict in the case of *Slovak pensions XVII*,[5] where it completely refused the view of Court of Justice and proclaimed its ruling in the *Landtová* case as an ultra vires decision (Zbíral 2012 or Král 2013). The dispute was finally resolved by the intervention of the executive power and a change in the Czech regulations. Notwithstanding that, the judicial conflict remains and could at least have theoretical consequences (Bobek 2014).

The duality and heterarchy is in fact written in the genetic information of the EU. The EU's internal institutional structure itself includes this duality. It encompasses institutions which can—in order to ensure the division of power—be seen as rivals of the Member States, namely the EU Commission and the Court of Justice (the sign of suppression of sovereignty) and it also contains institutions representing the interests of the Member States, namely the Council and European Council (a sign of an appreciation of sovereignty). What is more, plurality and heterarchy are even encoded in EU primary law. Article 4 paragraph 2, 3 TEU codifies mutual loyalty as well as mutual respect between supranational and national level.[6] It serves as the underframe for the further development of the effective application of EU law (it is well known that the principle of indirect effect was based on the Member State's commitment of loyalty) but on the other hand it could serve as the ultimate shield of Member States' important constitutional values, including the essence of their sovereignty (Grinc and Ondřejková 2014).

In the absence of a pyramidal structure of a legal system, when there is no established formal hierarchy between the EU and national law, and when every component of the system still wishes to assume primacy, we have to accept the existence of some grey zone between these actors (and their legal systems).

[4]Landtová, C-399/09, ECLI:EU:C:2011:415.

[5]Slovak Pensions XVII, PL. ÚS 5/12, ECLI:CZ:US:2012:Pl.US.5.12.1.

[6]Article 4, paragraph 2, 3 TEU states that: […] The Union shall respect the equality of Member States before the Treaties as well as their national identities, inherent in their fundamental structures, political and constitutional, inclusive of regional and local self-government. […] Pursuant to the principle of sincere cooperation, the Union and the Member States shall, in full mutual respect, assist each other in carrying out tasks which flow from the Treaties […].

3.2 The Area of Darkness?

Above-mentioned grey zone was designated as an 'area of darkness' (Cruz 2011). This darkness and related lack of enclosure contributes to a reduced comprehensibility of legal regulation and the erosion of law in its traditional understanding as the normative bound of society. The comfort of one legal system as a reflection of one sovereign's will is fading away. The pyramidal structure of the legal system was connected with the faith that an individual would be able to reach the ultimate norm that is associated with an unquestionable legitimacy. Indeed, the acceptance of several coexisting legal systems and power networks (Kysela 2014) undermines this certainty. Thus the tradition and automatic (somehow intuitive) acceptance of legal norms is endangered.

But it is not necessary to be so pessimistic. The aforementioned grey zone can also be perceived in a positive way. There is no need to approach the problem in a monistic attitude and argue in favour of any primacy being disrespectful, whether European or national. The grey zone gives us good ground for flexibility and openness. Czech professor of jurisprudence and former Judge of the Constitutional Court, Holländer (2009), argues against the phenomenon of reductionism in social sciences. He criticizes negligent one-sidedness, the tendency to find ultimate solutions, and wants to provoke interest in a plurality of default principles. We have to give it a try even when facing the challenge of integration. Postmodernity brings deconstruction. The nation state as the traditional security of stability is no longer above everything but somewhere in the middle (Bárány 2007). As Allan Cranston reminds us: 'Centuries ago, Copernicus taught humanity that the world is not the centre of the universe. Now humanity is learning that the nation-state is not the centre of the world' (Cranston 2004). The phenomenon of European integration, its federalizing tendencies and dominance of European law, essentially bring up the question of whether the Member States continue to possess their own sovereign status or not. My argument is that obviously they are still sovereigns. On the other hand their sovereignty has changed. And for this case we need to look for a new understanding of this concept and try to redefine its features (Jirásková 1999).

3.3 Sovereignty Still Matters, but It Is not the Same

The phenomena of legal heterarchy and postmodern pluralism opens the debates about a world without sovereignty ('beyond sovereignty, post sovereignty'), where neither state nor supranational organization is master. Neil MacCormick presents this view as an alternative to the classical 'recreative' concept of sovereignty, according to which loss of the sovereignty at one level inevitably leads to its recreation at another (MacCormick 1999). Contrary to this old perception, he argues that we should understand sovereignty as a category, which disappears without compensation once a state participates in an integration project. In this view, states are no longer sovereign, but they also are not subordinate to any other sovereign entity. He compares state sovereignty to virginity, which cannot be renewed after it is lost, but also no one else acquires it. Then he rejects both 'mega-sovereignty' of the EU and tens of 'polycentric' state sovereignties across Europe. Neil MacCormick also welcomes a world beyond sovereignty mainly because of the past bloody consequences of the classical 'sovereignty games' between states. He claims that: 'One of the main upshots of universal sovereign statehood was two disasters—world wars' and continues by asking whether: 'we [can] think of a world in which our normative existence and our practical life are anchored in, or related to, a variety of institutional systems, each of which has validity or operation in relation to some range of concerns, none of which is absolute over all the others, and all of which, for most purposes, can operate without serious mutual conflict in areas of overlap? If this is as possible practically as it clearly is conceptually, it would involve diffusion of political power centres as well as of legal authorities. It would depend on a high degree of relatively willing co-operation and a relatively low degree of coercion in its direct and naked forms. It would create space for a real and serious debate about the demands of subsidiarity' (MacCormick 1993).

Even though this optimistic view is very attractive and encompasses a deep message of humanity (or rather belief in humankind), it is hardly acceptable in the real world. A positive response to this question anticipates that we accept a common core of both the supranational and national legal systems. Shared values (Kumm 2005), common language, or approach to legal interpretation (Maduro 2003) could lead to the reception of a (post) sovereignty condition. But this theory seems, however, rather like a laboratory solution with minor significance in real life, as it places such great demand on both theory and practice.

It seems more suitable to describe the current state of affairs by using the term 'late sovereignty' (Walker 2002) rather than 'beyond sovereignty'. The above-mentioned perspective and call to abandon the concept of sovereignty faces another specific difficulty, particularly in connection with the Czech Republic and other countries of the former eastern bloc. Experience with the fact of the Brezhnev doctrine, which represented the actual suppression of autonomy in so-called Soviet satellites, led to the special constitutional accentuation of state sovereignty in these countries. Newly regained freedom became an important constitutional value (Halász 2001; Tokár 2001) and sensitive political question (Aziz 2004). Therefore it was anticipated that the new Member States and their constitutional authorities would be much more careful and much more sensitive about the loss or weakening of their sovereignty in connection with European integration than their Western counterparts (Sadurski 2006). Once the Czech Constitution states in article 1 paragraph 1, that 'The Czech Republic is a sovereign, unitary and democratic, law-abiding State, based on respect for the rights and freedoms of man and citizen', it is hard to imagine that, within the European Union, this constitutional feature could disappear! Acceptation of a state of affairs beyond sovereignty would mean an inadmissible negation of the explicit wording of the Constitution. For this reason, we have to accept the concept of state sovereignty as still valid but make an attempt to reconcile it with the ambitions of the European integration project.

Carl Schmitt reminds us that, among all concepts of legal and political theory, sovereignty is one that depends mostly on current and particular interests (Schmitt 1985). Czech constitutionalist and Judge of the Constitutional Court Jan Filip add that no interpretation of sovereignty can ever satisfy everyone (Filip 2009). Looking for an answer to the dilemma of how to grasp the concept of sovereignty within European integration seems to be a never-ending story. But one need not be so sceptical. It is the role and duty of scholarship to offer certain answers and solutions. The research objective of this paper is to analyze what implications for its national sovereignty arise from the membership of the Czech Republic in the EU. The outcome should be the harmonization of Czech statehood (and the constitutional requirement articulated in article 1 paragraph 1 of the Constitution) with participation in the European integration project. We have to look for paths of theoretical reconciliation and new definitions. European integration calls for new concepts and the modern shaping of the contours of the state sovereignty both in the field of constitutional theory as well as in the field of political science.

There are obviously some critical voices that reject new definitions. The attempts to find new definitions and content are sometimes being compared to the occult practices of fortune tellers more than serious scholarly work (Kurtulus 2005). I must reject that criticism. As Neil MacCormick wrote that, to understand a new legal reality which results from the development of supranational entities, a certain amount of imagination is needed (MacCormick 1999). The picture which is appearing in front of our eyes is an image of the European Union as a complex constitutional system. The concept of complexity in connection with the supranational system reflects both its meanings. It is a comprehensive, internally structured, system, as well as a system exhibiting a certain degree of difficulty that complicates its understanding. It might be determined as the 'constitutional mosaic' (Walker et al. 2011). And, yes, in looking for the new definitions, we have to walk a path of uncertain, even mythological character. It is no surprise that great revolutions in EU law (the establishment of principles of direct effect and primacy) were connected with the emergence of 'mythical' terminology. In the early days of integration, transcendent terms like 'founding fathers' and 'spirit of Treaties' were introduced as important arguments in favour of supranational constitutionalization (Cruz 2011). And it is worth saying that the outcomes based on those 'not scholarly' arguments were widely accepted at the time of their creation (Stein 1981) and over decades of practice.

References

Aziz, M. (2004). *The impact of European Rights on the National Legal Cultures*. Oxford: Hart Publishing.

Bárány, E. (2007). *Pojmy dobrého práva [The notion of good law]*. Bratislava: Eurokódex.

Bárány, E. (2009). Funkcionálna suverenita? In A. Gerloch & J. Wintr (Eds.), *Lisabonská smlouva a ústavní pořádek ČR* (pp. 115–119). Plzeň: Aleš Čeněk.

Bobek, M. (2014). Landtova, Holubec, and the problem of an uncooperative court: Implications for the preliminary ruling procedure. *EuConst, 10*(1), 54–89.

Borowski, M. (2008). Neil MacCormick's legal reconstruction of the European Community—Sovereignty and Legal Pluralism. In A.J. Menéndez, & J.E. Fossum, (Eds). *The post-sovereign constellation. Law and democracy in Neil D. MacCormick's legal and political theory* (pp. 191–231). Oslo: Arena.

Brinkhorst, L. J. (2009). National sovereignty in the EU: An outdated concept. In M. Bulterman et al. (Eds). *Views of European law from the mountain. Liber Amicorum piet jan slot* (pp. 327–333). Alphen aan den Rijn: Kluwer Law International.

Cranston, A. (2004). *The sovereignty revolution.* Stanford: Stanford University Press.

Cruz, J. B. (2011). An area of darkness: Three Conceptions of the relationship between European Union Law and State Constitutional Law. In N. Walker, J. Shaw, & S. Tierney (Eds.), *Europe's constitutional Mosaic* (pp. 49–71). Oxford: Hart Publishing.

Filip, J. (2009). Senátní návrh na zahájení řízení a nález k Lisabonské smlouvě: Procesní aspekty [Senate's proposal for the review of treaty of Lisbon: Procedural aspects]. In A. Gerloch & J. Wintr (Eds.), *Lisabonská smlouva a ústavní pořádek ČR [Treaty of Lisbon and constitutional order of the Czech Republic]* (pp. 29–47). Plzeň: Aleš Čeněk.

Forejtová, M. (2013). *Diskriminace jako referenční kritérium v judikatuře evropských soudů [Discrimination as a reference in the case law of the European courts].* Plzeň: Aleš Čeněk.

Grimm, D., & Bydžovská, Z. (2010). Interview. Euroskop.cz. https://www.euroskop.cz/8801/17387/clanek/staty-ztratily-monopol-na-legitimni-nasili/. Accessed 20 Sep 2015.

Grinc, J., & Ondřejková, J. (2014). The state and the European Union. In J. Kysela (Ed.), *State as a giant with feet of clay* (pp. 61–100). Frankfurt am Main: Peter Lang GmbH.

Halász, I. (2001). Spoločenské a ústavné súvislosti národnej suverenity a európskej integrácie v Maďarskej republike [Societal and constitutional implications of the National Sovereignty and European Integration in Hungary]. In D. Lengyelová (Ed.), *Teoretickoprávne súvislosti vstupu suverénneho štátu do Európskej únie [Theoretical implications of the accession of Sovereign State to the EU]* (pp. 101–110). Bratislava: Slovak Academic Press.

Holländer, P. (2009). *Filipika proti redukcionizmu [Filipica against reductionism].* Bratislava: Kalligram.

Jirásková, V. (1999). Ústavní základ, na jakém se členské státy vzdaly svých kompetencí a způsob jejích předání EU [Constitutional foundations and methods of transfer of State competences to the EU]. In V. Pavlíček (Ed). *Suverenita a evropská integrace. K ústavněprávním souvislostem vstupu České republiky do Evropské unie* [Sovereignty and European integration. On the constitutional aspects of the accession of the Czech Republic to the EU]. (pp. 49–70). Praha: Univerzita Karlova.

Král, R. (2013). Questioning the recent challenge of the Czech Constitutional Court to the Court of Justice. *European Public Law, 19*(2), 271–280.

Kumm, M. (2005). The Jurisprudence of constitutional conflict: Constitutional supremacy in Europe before and after the constitutional treaty. *European Law Journal, 11*(3), 262–307.

Kurtulus, E. (2005). *State sovereignty. Concept, phenomenon and ramifications.* New York: Palgrave Macmillan.

MacCormick, N. (1993). Beyond the Sovereign State. *The Modern Law Review, 56*(1), 1–18.

Kysela, J. (2014). *State as a giant with feet of clay.* Frankfurt am Main: Peter Lang GmbH.

MacCormick, N. (1999). *Questioning sovereignty. Law, state, and nation in the European Commonwealth.* New York: Oxford University Press.

Maduro, M. P. (1998). *We the court. The European Court of Justice and the European Economic Constitution. A critical reading of article 30 of the EC treaty.* Portland: Hart Publishing.

Maduro, M. P. (2003). Contrapunctual law: Europe's constitutional Pluralism in Action. In N. Walker (Ed.), *Sovereignty in transition* (pp. 201–237). Oxford: Hart Publishing.

Meunier, S., & McNamara, K. (2007). *Making history: European integration and institutional change at Fifty.* Oxford: Oxford University Press.

Pavlíček, V. et al. (2011). *Ústavní právo a státověda, II. díl* [Constitutional law and theory of state, 2nd part]. Praha: Leges.

Přibáň, J. (2013). Ranní červánky globálního konstitucionalismu: O "radostné" právní vědě v postnacionální společnosti [Morning alpenglow of global constitutionalism: The "joyful" legal science in the post-national society]. *Právník, 152*(2), 105–123.

Sadurski, W. (2006). 'Solange, chapter 3': Constitutional Courts in Central Europe—Democracy—European Union. *EUI working paper Law no.* 40.

Schmitt, C. (1985). *Political theology: Four chapters on the concept of sovereignty*. Cambridge, Massachusetts: The MIT Press.

Schorkopf, F. (2009). The European Union as An Association of Sovereign States: Karlsruhe's ruling on the treaty of Lisbon. *German Law Journal, 10*(8), 1219–1240.

Stein, E. (1981). Lawyers, Judges, and the Making of a Transnational Constitution. *The American Journal of International Law, 75*(1), 1–27.

Stein, E. (1999). *Thoughts from a bridge. A retrospective of Writings on New Europe and American Fedealism*. Ann Arbor: University of Michigan Press.

Tokár, A. (2001). Suverenita a rozširovanie Európskej únie po summite v Nice [Sovereignty and the enlargement of the EU adter nice summit]. *Právny obzor, 84*(3), 197–205.

Večeřa, M. (2001) Legalita a demokratická legitimita v podmínkách eurointegrace [Legality and democratic legitimacy on the background of European integration]. In D. Lengyelová [Ed.], *Teoretickoprávne súvislosti vstupu suverénneho štátu do Európskej únie* [Theoretical implications of the accession of Sovereign state to the EU] (pp. 17–25). Bratislava: Slovak Academic Press.

Walker, N. (2002). The idea of constitutional Pluralism. *Modern Law Review, 65*(3), 317–359.

Walker, N. (2006). The migration of constitutional ideas and the migration of the constitutional idea: The case of the EU. In S. Choudhry, S. (Ed.). *The migration of constitutional ideas* (pp. 316–343). New York: Cambridge University Press.

Walker, N., et al. (2011). *Europe's Constitutional Mosaic*. Oxford and Portland: Hart Publishing.

Zbíral, R. (2012). Czech Constitutional Court, judgment of 31 January 2012, Pl. ÚS 5/12. A Legal revolution or negligible episode? Court of Justice decision proclaimed ultra vires. *Common Market Law Review, 49*(4), 1475–1492.

Chapter 4
Sovereignty Vis-á-Vis Moloch of European Integration

4.1 Two Perspectives on the Meaning of State Sovereignty

When defining the term state sovereignty, we come across a constitutional evergreen—a conflict between doctrines which consider this concept a unitary and practically indivisible 'artefact', and theories which believe that sovereignty is divisible and, thus, that we can use its various parts. In other words, conflict over the question of whether state sovereignty is an indivisible quality or a divisible capital.[1] Michal Bartoň accurately sees this conflict as a clash between a binary view, i.e. yes/no understanding and viewing sovereignty as a rating scale concept, i.e. more/less understanding (Bartoň 2010).

4.1.1 *Static Perception*

The first view is static and étatic. It is known as the traditional or 'Westphalian' understanding of sovereignty. Sovereignty is defined as an immanent characteristic of a state, and no other unit, higher or lower, can become a sovereign but a state. This approach makes the stabilization aspect of sovereignty more than obvious. Sovereignty is an axiomatic category due to its indivisible and non-transferable quality. When a state ceases to exist, its sovereignty also ends. And, contrarily, it emerges when a new state comes into a being. The existence of a plurality of sovereign structures on one territory is in this approach unthinkable. German

This chapter is based on my article with the title Lessons from the 'Constitutional Mythology' or How to Reconcile the Concepts of State with European Integration which was published in DANUBE: Law and Economics Review (see references Hamuľák 2015).

[1]Or, in other words, 'Indivisible Quality or a Divisible Property' (Kurtulus 2005).

O. Hamuľák, *National Sovereignty in the European Union*,
SpringerBriefs in Law, DOI 10.1007/978-3-319-45351-4_4

Federal Constitutional Court Judge Udo di Fabio, who represents this understanding of sovereignty, notes that sovereignty is a concept of international law and actually means state independence. In his view, one is either independent or not. It is exactly the same as with freedom. In international law, states cannot hand over sovereignty because then they would no longer be states. He therefore recognizes that visions of divided or shared sovereignty are misleading.[2] Within such a traditional understanding, sovereignty is a category which does not alter its content or structure. It can only change its holder. The transfer of sovereignty to another subject means that the original holder loses it. Sovereignty is absolute; a sovereign is a single entity (new states in the case of dissolution, federation in the case of unification, a current state legally joined by an originally sovereign entity). This perspective works on the assumption that there are winners and losers. Accepting a new (another) sovereign simultaneously means accepting the demise of one's own original sovereignty. Even the German Federal Constitutional Court rejects the flexible character of sovereignty and sticks to its traditional understanding (Tomushat 2009). German Federal Constitutional Court in its Lisbon judgement presented the view according to which there was no division or sharing of sovereignty between the EU and its Member States. The EU did not possess its own sovereignty; it is understood as a representative and executor of Member States' original competences. The German Federal Constitutional Court resumed here its 'Maastricht' doctrine and understanding of the EU as an association of states (*Europäischen Staatenverbund*). States continue to be sole and final sovereign subjects. According to German Federal Constitutional Court, the EU cannot exist as a sovereign next to its Member States. If one day the EU would like to transform itself to a state subject and sovereign entity, it would always be according to the German Federal Constitutional Court at the expense of its Member States. The EU would work as their successor. In this respect, the Court pointed out that neither the current state of EU primary law nor the current form of Basic Law allowed such transformation.[3]

When we apply above-mentioned perspective to the circumstances of European integration, we can come to two different results. If we accept that the EU is a new sovereign, we would also have to negate sovereign statehood and the further independent existence of the Member States. This view is clearly unacceptable. The EU has not become a superstate which would absorb its Member States. They are still here as (the original) sovereigns. The obligation to ratify every important reform of primary law and general right of supervision over any Treaty revision places the responsibility for the destiny of integration into the hands of these states. As the German Federal Constitutional Court noted in its decision on the Euro

[2]See transcript of the interview with Udo di Fabio from 12 December, 2009. Euroskop.cz. Retrieved from http://www.euroskop.cz/8801/14887/clanek/po-lisabonu-jsme-uz-na-hranici-federace. 11 See the Federal Constitutional Court's judgement of 7 September, 2011, Euro-Urteil, 2 BvR 987/10, 2 BvR 1485/10, 2 BvR 1099/10.

[3]See German Federal Constitutional Court judgment of 30 June 2009, 2 BvE 2/08 Lissabon-Urteil, points 224 and 231.

Rescue Package, Germany (and we may transplant this to all Member States in general) is not subject to any unpredictable automatism of EU integration, which would follow only its own course irrespective of the Member States, but diversely it as a Master of the Treaty is responsible for such changes. On the other hand, if we were to assert that the states are the only and exclusive possessors of sovereignty, we would then reject the fact that the EU is more than just an international intergovernmental organization, that it is an independent subject with its own constitutional story and own responsibility.

Some political views will continue to perceive EU membership as a threat to state sovereignty while others will see it as its materialization or even reinforcement (Heartfield 2007). The EU's internal institutional structure itself includes this duality because it contains institutions which can—in order to ensure division of power—be seen as rivals of the Member States—namely the EU Commission and the Court of Justice (suppression of sovereignty) and it also contains institutions representing the interests of the Member States—Council and European Council (appreciation of sovereignty).

Theoretical approaches should, however, abandon these political evaluations and should try to offer solutions, a clear perspective on the content of the concept of sovereignty and its understanding in the context of EU membership. As described by Pavel Holländer when discussing the changes in our understanding of the concept of modern state: ': It is high time [...] to try to interpret altered historical reality in concepts' (Holländer 2013). Opinions that the state continues to be the only absolute sovereign, that EU membership does not affect our understanding of state sovereignty, or that the EU is only one of many forms of an interstate cooperation without inner autonomy, resembles to the closing eyes to reality like in the Anderson's Emperor's New Clothes.[4]

4.1.2 *Dynamic Approach*

The second approach considers sovereignty to be a flexible category (materially and functionally). It allows for some division and transfer of its parts. According to this view, we see acceptance of shared sovereignty and a formation of its pooled form. Sovereignty partially passes away from states and can be assigned (in a partial, limited understanding) to other, e.g. supranational, entities. Neil Walker notes that we may understand authority and sovereignty in the post-Westphalian order as non-exclusive terms. He adds that loss of exclusivity does not necessarily lead to a loss of autonomy (Walker 2002).

[4]'So off went the Emperor in procession under his splendid canopy. Everyone in the streets and the windows said, "Oh, how fine are the Emperor's new clothes! Don't they fit him to perfection? And see his long train!" Nobody would confess that he couldn't see anything, for that would prove him either unfit for his position, or a fool'.

A new perspective on sovereignty appears mainly in the last decade of the twentieth century after the fall of the Iron Curtain and is undoubtedly connected with the processes of globalization as well (Agnew 2009). In this regard Sajó predicted that the first two decades of the new millennium would increasingly demand that nation states give up their national sovereignty (Sajó 2001). The interdependence of world economies, global environmental and security threats, international terrorism, real power of multinational corporations, the parallel world of cyberspace and many other external factors further intensified the deconstruction of traditional state structures (Ušiak 2009). Globalization requires a new understanding of the role that states play. Their power is suppressed by public as well as private factors. Václav Havel in some public statements aptly observed that, for example, accepting a foreign military base on a country's territory would not affect a state's sovereignty any more than selling shares of strategic national companies to a foreign shareholder (Šamalík 2008).

The second alternative reading of sovereignty—the so-called rating scale concept—is an ideal tool for reacting to the challenges of European integration and for opening up the old concept to new situations. Since the end of the Thirty Years' War, we have somehow become accustomed to a Europe where nation states dominated and were unwavering holders of absolute sovereignty. We consider the modern state to be some ontological (or even mythical) being whose existence does not need to be proven (Wind 2003). We have also become accustomed to the idea that everything arises from a nation state—society, public power, authority, legal regulation, etc. However, we should be reminded that the concept of state sovereignty is not eternal. It was only introduced some four or five hundred years ago. But European history precedes Bodin and the Westphalian system. European history had been defined by the pluralism and heterarchy of two swords (ecclesiastical and secular) as its two power centres for many centuries (Goldman 2007). And the presence of these two centres had not in any way negated the existence of state structures—medieval kingdoms.

Moreover, sovereignty cannot be understood as a static concept that has not changed its content and definition over the years. Over the centuries, the internal dimension of sovereignty has been weakened by the democratization of societies, by seeking the sources of legitimate power, by enforcing the concept of a material constitutional state (Merriam 1900). Its external dimension has been modified in connection with deepening international collaboration and integration, with the introduction of international rules for conflict resolution, with the establishment of integration bodies, etc. (Holländer 2009b). The concept of sovereignty itself is a theoretical construction reacting to some specific political fact. The historical roots of the traditional (Bodinian) understanding of sovereignty can be found in Western Europe in the early modern period, when the concept of sovereignty became a tool of secularization, the sword defending the power of the kings against papal omnipotence and a tool emancipating nation states from the emperor's power (Hobza 1933). The concept of (monarch's) sovereignty was born from the blood of the St. Bartholomew's Day Massacre (1572) and became the foundation for the organization of governance in a modern state (Beaulac 2003). The legal construction of absolute and everlasting king's sovereignty was a prerequisite for a state's existence, a requirement for its internal organization and stability. Centralism and absolutism became the foundations of the early modern state and a tool for overcoming power entropy, eliminating so-called states within states and feudal fragmentation (Klokočka 2006).

However, the understanding of sovereignty further developed in the following periods and flexibly reacted to historical changes. The most distinct change related to the holders of sovereignty. We may interconnect the sovereignty holder with the emancipation revolutions—the monarch's emancipation from the Pope and the emperor (sixteenth/seventeenth centuries), the people's emancipation from the monarch (eighteenth century), the emancipation of nations/nation states (nineteenth century) and the emancipation of individuals/human rights holders from the state power apparatus (20th century). States (sovereigns) are now increasingly expected to serve their citizens. This responsibility leads to a new understanding of internal sovereignty and concepts of so-called Ethical Sovereignty (Minkkinen 2007).

Another tendency to adopt an open understanding of sovereignty results from the development of new forms of organization and the managing of social relations in an integrated Europe. Indeed, sovereignty continues to be a constitutional concept indispensable for the constitutional organization of society (Rabkin 2007). It anchors the behaviour of specific subjects with authority, legitimacy, responsibility and accountability. But it needs redefinition when considered in connection with European integration. It is indispensable to reflect the social developments and new phenomena by hermeneutical shifts. In the specific conditions of European integration, sovereignty cannot handle traditional perspectives. The application of a modern viewpoint allows us to escape a theoretical gridlock known as 'the Brunner Paradox'. This paradox refers to the conflict between the practical acceptation of specific features of European integration on the one hand and the application of old language and static constitutional reasoning on the other, a practice traditionally interconnected with the 'European decisions' of the German Federal Constitutional Court (Everson 1998).

Textbook understanding of sovereignty in its traditional meaning considers this concept as an expression of the highest, unique, independent and unconditional power, controlling a certain territory and the population living there. The negative aspect of sovereignty is independence, non-conditionality on any other power. Positive aspect of sovereignty (sovereign power) is its exclusiveness, i.e. elimination of any other power, respectively its impact on the same territory. Sovereignty is in this view is generally described as an independent, exclusive and unlimited power (Svatoň 2007). This traditional Westphalian understanding of sovereignty is sometimes used as an argument against the deepening of European integration (Klaus 2012). But in real life this abstract sovereignty (unique, highest, independent power) does not obstruct the perpetual development of the European project. All Member States have actually accepted the specific nature of the EU and the new legal situation. The founding Member States did it once they provided the EC/EU with a 'self-constituting' programme. And all acceding Member States did it by deliberate acceptation of the up-to-date developed supranational constitutionalism.[5] In connection with countries of Central Europe, Jiří Přibáň openly states that these countries had sold out their newly acquired sovereignty in exchange for their return to Europe (Přibáň 2006).

4.1.3 Reshaped but Still Present—Preserving Sovereignty in the Ideal World of Concepts

The institute of state sovereignty had undergone a transformation and gained new proportion. It is no longer solely an attribute of a nation state and an expression of its power over the controlled territory. The current concept of sovereignty is necessarily connected with the state's willingness and will to participate in venues of international cooperation, and to share its competences with other subjects of the international community. Sovereignty is a 'manifestation of the new order in a globalized world'[6] where economies and decision-making processes become interdependent and some responsibility has shifted from the national states to another centres of governance. As a consequence, new approaches to traditional theoretical concepts emerge (Zemánek 2009). One of them, state sovereignty, acquires a new dimension in connection with European integration, where sharing common goals and more importantly sharing competences gave rise to concepts of shared (Wallace 1999) or pooled (Williams 1990) sovereignty. The dividing (and pooling) of sovereignty is a reaction to the formation of a 'post national global society' (Přibáň 2012). This obviously inspired CCC and became the core of its argumentation: 'The European Union has advanced by far the furthest in the concept of pooled sovereignty, and today is creating an entity sui generis, which is difficult to classify in classical political science categories. It is more a linguistic question whether to describe the integration process as a'loss' of part of sovereignty, or competences, or, somewhat more fittingly, as, e.g., 'lending, ceding' of part of the competence of a sovereign. It may seem paradoxical that they key expression of state sovereignty is the ability to dispose of one's sovereignty (or part of it), or to temporarily or even permanently cede certain competences.'[7]

Today, a sovereign should be well able to organize the performance of the society, to tolerate the realms of fragmentation, integration and globalization. Sovereignty expresses the state's capability to secure social needs and protect individuals in a global context. A state is not sovereign because it holds the highest, unique and absolute power over a certain territory and its population. It is sovereign because it preserves a minimal pool of instruments necessary to protect the interests and needs of its population. A state's sovereignty is not threatened by the transfer of

[5]First enlargement in 1973 came almost exactly ten years after the famous verdicts in *Van Gend en Loos* and *Costa* judgements.

[6]Treaty of Lisbon I, Pl. ÚS 19/08, ECLI:CZ:US:2008:Pl.US.19.08.1, point 102.

[7]Treaty of Lisbon I, Pl. ÚS 19/08, ECLI:CZ:US:2008:Pl.US.19.08.1, point 104.

some competences to the EU level and the acceptance of its influence. Contrary to that, it would be threatened if the states lost their ability to serve the good of their society and its components, no matter if individually or integrated in the common polity.

The concept of the sharing of competences between Member States and the EU based on voluntary participation represents a foundation for deviation from the traditional closed understanding of state sovereignty. EU membership and the concept of shared/pooled sovereignty also carry many advantages for the Member States. CCC reminds us that Member States should accept a sum of obligations and respect established formal processes because they (voluntarily) participate in the construction of the European supranational entity and make use of its advantages. It specifically states that: '[…] in a modern democratic state governed by the rule of law, the sovereignty of the state is not an aim in and of itself, that is, in isolation, but is a means for fulfilling the fundamental values on which the construction of a democratic state governed by the rule of law stands […] the transfer of certain state competences, that arises from the free will of the sovereign, and will continue to be exercised with the sovereign's participation in a manner that is agreed upon in advance and is subject to review, is not a conceptual weakening of sovereignty, but, on the contrary, can lead to strengthening it within the joint actions of an integrated whole'.[8]

States do not lose their sovereignty by pooling it. They only shift the responsibility for political decisions to a supranational authority and to some extent trade the capability to produce individual solutions for the advantage of higher effectiveness within the bounds of a common project (Lake 2007). Member States formed a new sovereign entity, with which they share a common territory on which it executes its power (Forsyth 1995). The relationship between the EU and its Member States is not connected by a splitting of sovereignty but by the overlapping sovereign competences of both.

A flexible perception of sovereignty in the ideal world of concepts allows Member States to preserve their sovereignty vis-á-vis European integration. Committing some of their original competences to the supranational institutions does not lead to a loss or depreciation of sovereignty. On the contrary, the collective management of issues of common interest strengthens it. Sovereignty is responsibility connected with the duty to preserve the good of society and rights of individuals. CCC stressed this point also in its evaluation of the EU Charter of Fundamental Rights vis-á-vis national standards of human rights protection in its first Lisbon ruling. Legally binding Charter was not understood as attack on the Czech constitutionality or more precisely Czech sovereignty. CCC stressed the added value of EU Charter, its importance for legitimizing of the EU's decision-making processes and material conformity between Charter and national standards of protection of fundamental rights: '[…] EU Charter is in harmony not only with the material core of the Constitution, but also with all provisions of the

[8]Treaty of Lisbon II, Pl. ÚS 29/09, ECLI:CZ:US:2009:Pl.US.29.09.3, point 147.

constitutional order. […] the European institutional guarantee of the standard of protection of human rights and fundamental freedoms to be compatible with the standard ensured on the basis of the constitutional order of the Czech Republic. […]'.[9] But it is worth to mention here that stated material conformity was declared only from the abstract point of view. Pluralistic notion postulates the best guarantee for the human rights and for that reason CCC stressed that in future it will follow those standards which shall offer the highest rank of protection for individual whatever source they come from. Considering this 'ultimate good' solution it is possible to think about preference of both national and EU standards over each other according to specific situation. In the case of lack of protection on the Union level CCC anticipated the possibility to take over transferred competencies by the Czech Republic: '[…] the leading principle in the area of human rights and fundamental freedoms is the most effective possible protection of the individual, together with the clear enforceability of the rights directly on the basis of catalogues of human rights, usually without the intermediation of other legal texts of lower legal force. […]'.[10]

Last but not least the concept of responsible sovereign is connected also with the institute of sanction regime against the Member State anticipated in article 7 TEU. Here in connection with potential sanctions against Czech Republic for alleged violations of human rights as fundamental principles on which EU is based it need to be said, that CCC continue in its inductive approach based on the accentuation of the role of the states as building stones of the Union. According to this notion there is (from material point of view) nothing new on the Union's level. Union standards are built on the common base of national constitutional rules and traditions. From this point of view there is no risk of attack on sovereignty in case of imposition of sanction under article 7 of the TEU because state actions which might be evaluated as breach of EU human rights standard will be *ipso iure* in discordance with Czech constitutional standards, too. According to the CCC: '[…] the opportunity to suspend the rights that arise to a Member State from the Treaties cannot mean a violation of the fundamental characteristic of the Czech Republic as a sovereign, unitary and democratic state governed by the rule of law […] because this is a penalty only vis-à-vis a Member State that violates the values on which the European Union is founded; these values, as stated above, are also among the fundamental principles protected by the Constitution of the Czech Republic. If the Czech Republic observes its own constitutional order, suspension of the rights arising to it from membership in the EU does not come into consideration. […]'.[11] As the sovereign is limited by Constitution itself, the same limitation (materially) by the EU sanction regime cannot be understood as the breach of state sovereignty either.

[9]Treaty of Lisbon I, Pl. ÚS 19/08, ECLI:CZ:US:2008:Pl.US.19.08.1, point 197.

[10]Treaty of Lisbon I, Pl. ÚS 19/08, ECLI:CZ:US:2008:Pl.US.19.08.1, point 198.

[11]Treaty of Lisbon I, Pl. ÚS 19/08, ECLI:CZ:US:2008:Pl.US.19.08.1, point 209.

References

Agnew, J. (2009). *Globalization and sovereignty*. Lanham: Rowman & Littlefield Publishers.

Bartoň, M. (2010). Lisabonská smlouva a rozhodnutí ústavního soudu ČR: otázka suverenity státu [Treaty of Lisbon and the decision of the Czech constitutional court]. In J. Jirásek, et al. (Eds.), *Konstytucyjno-prawne aspekty czlonkostwa Rzeczypospolitej Polskiej i Republiki Czeskiej v Unii Europejsiej [Constitutional aspects of the membership of Poland and Czech Republic in the EU]* (pp. 137–139). Bydgoszcz: Wydawnictwo KPSW.

Beaulac, S. (2003). Le Pouvoir sémiologique du mot „Souveraineté" dans l'oeuvre de Bodin. *International Journal for the Semiotics of Law-Revue Internationale deSémiotique Juridique*, *16*(1), 45–76.

Everson, M. (1998). Beyond the *Bundesverfassungsgericht*: On the Necessary cunning of constitutional reasoning. *European Law Journal*, *4*(4), 389–410.

Forsyth, M. (1995). *Political science, federalism and Europe*. Leicester: University of Leicester.

Goldman, B. D. (2007). *Globalisation and the Western legal tradition. Recurring patterns of law and authority*. Cambridge: Cambridge University Press.

Hamuľák, O. (2015). Lessons from the "Constitutional Mythology" or How to reconcile the concepts of state with European integration, DANUBE: Law and Economics. *Review*, *6*(2), 75–90.

Heartfield, J. (2007). European Union: A process without a subject. In Ch. J. Bickerton et al. (eds). *Politics without sovereignty. A critique of contemporary international relations* (pp. 131–149). Oxon: University College London Press.

Hobza, A. (1933). *Úvod do mezinárodního práva mírového* [Introduction to the Public International Law]. Praha: 'self-published'.

Holländer, P. (2009). *Základy všeobecné státovědy [Introduction to the theory of state]*. Plzeň: Aleš Čeněk.

Holländer, P. (2013). Soumrak moderního státu [The twilight of modern state]. *Právník*, *152*(1), 1–28.

Klaus, V. (2012). *Europe: The shattering of illusions*. London: Bloomsbury Continuum.

Klokočka, V. (2006). *Ústavní systémy evropských států [Constitutional systems of European states]*. Praha: Linde.

Kurtulus, E. (2005). *State sovereignty. Concept, Phenomenon and ramifications*. New York: Palgrave Macmillan.

Lake, A. D. (2007). Delegating divisible sovereignty. Sweeping a conceptual minefield. *The Review of International Organizations*, *3*(2), 219–237.

Merriam, C. H. E. (1900). *History of the theory of sovereignty since Rousseau*. New York: Columbia University Press.

Minkkinen, P. (2007). The Ethos of sovereignty: A critical appraisal. *Human Rights Review*, *8*(2), 33–51.

Přibáň, J. (2006). Happy Returns to Europe? The Union's identity, constitution-making, and its impact on the Central European Accession States. In W. Sadurski, et al. (Eds.), *Spreading democracy and the rule of law?* (pp. 193–218). Dordrecht: Springer.

Přibáň, J. (2012). Vlast nebo domov? Česká otázka v postnacionální společnosti [Homeland of home? Czech question in post-national society]. Novinky.cz., http://www.novinky.cz/kultura/salon/282596-jiri-priban-vlast-nebo-domov.html. Accessed 20 December 2015.

Rabkin, J. A. (2007). *Law without nations? Why constitutional government requires Sovereign states*. Princeton: Princeton University Press.

Sajó, A. (2001). Constitutional law in twenty years from now. *Acta Juridica Hungarica*, *42*(3–4), 149–157.

Šamalík, F. (2008). *Ústava sevřená v protikladech restaurace*. [The constitution constricted by the paradoxes of restoration]. Praha: Masarykova dělnická akademie.

Svatoň, J. (2009). Suverenita státu [The sovereignty of state]. In J. Filip et al. *Základy státovědy* [The introduction to the theory of state] (p. 23). Brno: Masarykova univerzita.

Tomushat, Ch. (2009). The ruling of Geman constitutional court on the Lisbon treaty. *German Law Review, 10*(8), 1259–1261.
Ušiak, J. (2009). Premeny suverenity štátov v kontexte vybraných teórií medzinárodných vzťahov [The modalities of state sovereignty in the context of selected theories of international relations]. *Současná Evropa, 1*(2), 35–53.
Walker, N. (2002). The idea of constitutional Pluralism. *Modern Law Review, 65*(3), 317–359.
Wallace, W. (1999). The sharing of sovereignty: The European paradox. *Political Studies, 47*(3), 503–521.
Williams, S. (1990). Sovereignty and accountability in the European community. *The Political Quarterly, 61*(3), 299–317.
Wind, M. (2003). The European Union as a polycentric polity: Returning to a neo-medieval Europe? In J. H. H. Weiler & M. Wind (Eds.), *European Constitutionalism beyond the state* (pp. 103–131). Cambridge: Cambridge University Press.
Zemánek, J. (2009). Přezkum ústavnosti Lisabonské smlouvy: obsahové otázky [The constitutional review of treaty of Lisbon—Material questions]. *Jurisprudence, 18*(1), 32–41.

Chapter 5
Practical Sovereignty in a Real World—Relationship Between EU Law and National Law (The Czech Perspective)

Supranational law reaches its goals either through the effect of its own norms or through national law based on European rules. Thus, also the question of the relationship between European and national law (as a whole) must reflect these two options. To summarize the application of EU law to the legal system of a Member State can be of two different types

(a) Direct, normative influence on the national legal system, i.e. its enrichment with new 'European' norms,
(b) Indirect, value-based influence, when the goals of European integration, the ideological basis of the EU and its law, the intentions and purposes of the EU's legislator, etc. must be considered by national authorities when interpreting national law, i.e. it is enriched with new 'European' meanings.

The first type of influence is connected with the direct application of EU legal norms in national law or with the application of EU norms contained in national legislation, which transposes EU law. These types of EU legal effects open space for clashes between European and national law. There is a danger of a 'genuine conflict' between the national and EU norms. It is because two different norms stemming from independent legal systems can potentially apply to an identical situation. Because these norms originate in different (independent) legal systems, none of the traditional imperative relationships of supremacy (*lex superior derogat legi inferiori*), temporality (*lex posterior derogat legi priori*), or speciality (*lex specialis derogat legi generali*) apply.

The resolution of the relationship between these norms under such circumstances depends on the extent and will of national authorities to apply or rather accept the principle of primacy of EU law over national law (as the Court of Justice perceives it).

The second type covers the indirect effects when the implementing authority does not face the dilemma of choosing between the national and EU norm, yet it also struggles with challenges relevant to EU law. Specifically, the challenges are related to the existence of its obligation to interpret national law in line with the EU norm (EU-consistent interpretation). Here a possibility exists that tension between

O. Hamuľák, *National Sovereignty in the European Union*,
SpringerBriefs in Law, DOI 10.1007/978-3-319-45351-4_5

supranational and national law will arise especially when objectives of the EU norm which national authority should follow when interpreting national law is in breach with the requirements of the national law.

The Court of Justice claims that independent character, binding force and efficiency of EU norms require full and unitary application of EU law from the moment of its adoption and throughout its legal 'existence' in all Member States. The Court of Justice does not distinguish between EU and national laws in their application by national courts and public authorities. On the contrary, it establishes that the EU legal provisions are indispensable parts of the Member States' legal systems (see *Van Gen den Loos*; *Simmenthal* or *Melki and Abdeli* cases[1]). Direct (immediate) applicability includes a command for the national courts to accept supranational law as their own and apply it as originally adopted, i.e. without transposition into national law—this command is an expression of general obligation to apply (Prechal 2007) which binds the national institutions. National authorities must accept EU law as an integral part of their national legal system. But moreover they have to consider the content and objectives of the EU when interpreting national norms (principle of indirect effect).

Principles of direct and indirect effect build together the very wide arena for the penetration of the supranational regulation into the national practice. But once the normative ideas of the supranational legislator come into the effect in national practice the risk arises that they will get into the conflicts with concurring national norms, which forms another independent—national—system of law. To solve this clashes Court of Justice introduced another crucial principle of EU law—the principle of primacy.[2] According to that principle when a conflict between EU law and national law arises, national authorities need to give preference to the European norm and not apply the national one. The main principles of application clearly show that EU law behaves vis-á-vis national law as a dominant legal system. If the EU law collides with the wording or meaning of national norms, it is this dominance which resolves the problem and causes that conflicting national rules will not be applied or that national law will be interpreted in line with the EU law requirements.

The penetration of EU supranational law into the national legal systems disrupts the 'sovereignty idol'—the traditional concept providing that a direct intervention of external norms into the legal system of a sovereign state is inadmissible (Klokočka 2006). Thus, it is not surprising that in the landmark decision, which for the first time established the autonomy and internal effects of the EC law (*Van Gend en Loos*), the three opposing Member States (Germany, Belgium and the Netherlands), argued that sovereignty had to be preserved. In case of conflict between EU and national law, the national norm's applicability should be suppressed or its established interpretation abandoned. This implies that the effect of

[1]Van Gend en Loos, 26/62, ECLI:EU:C:1963:1; Simmenthal, 106/77, ECLI:EU:C:1978:49, Melki and Abdeli, C-188/10, ECLI:EU:C:2010:363.

[2]Flaminio Costa vs. ENEL, 6/64, ECLI:EU:C:1964:66.

national law is limited and the power of the sovereign that would otherwise possess monopoly over regulation of affected legal relationships is weakened. Wojciech Sadurski defines state sovereignty as based in preservation, respectively protection, of basic attributes of national constitutionality. He argues that sovereignty could be undermined if all national laws were subjected to the priority of EU law and the Member State's law would lose its autonomous core value (Sadurski 2006). This is the main question I will evaluate in the following chapters of this volume. The emphasis will be given to the perspective of Czech constitutional law.

5.1 Constitutional Limits of Normative Influence of EU Law

The answer to the question how to understand (in the world of ideal concepts) sovereignty of state participating in the integration project (evaluated in previous chapters) does not solve the problem of how to outline the borders of the newly defined sovereignty in the real world of relations between normatively autonomous legal systems. In this sub-chapter I will focus shortly on the reaction of the CCC to that supranational penetration and consequences for the 'sovereignty idol' mentioned above. In this respect, we might use the term practical sovereignty. This type of sovereignty is connected with the need to preserve the elementary attributes of constitutionality even in situation when state participates on a pluralist or hybrid model of public power represented by EU (Večeřa and Machalová 2010). The European Union or rather the expansion of EU law is kept in acceptable limits by elementary norms of constitutional order.

Along with the development of integration in Europe we have experienced power proliferation and the arrival of sovereignty surplus (Walker 2007), which led to a dissolve of responsibility and therefore brought a threat to the legitimacy of public power in Member States. The reaction of CCC to this development can be described as the relative acceptance of dominance of EU law, what allows CCC to preserve some considerable components of Czech constitutionality; thus, it meets the requirement of preserving practical sovereignty.

First of all we must mention that once dealing with the supranational requirements, CCC showed the pro-European attitude and acknowledged the autonomous character of EU law. In its seminal ruling *Sugar Quotas III*[3] it opened the Czech legal system to these principles opting for wide interpretation of the article 10a paragraph 1 of Czech Constitution.[4] The provision which strictly literally just empowers the Czech Republic to transfer some of competencies to the international

[3]Sugar Quotas III, Pl.ÚS 50/04, ECLI:CZ:US:2006:Pl.US.50.04.

[4]This provision states that: 'Certain powers of Czech Republic authorities may be transferred by treaty to an international organization or institution'.

bodies was interpreted by the CCC as 'two-way' provision which also serves as a constitutional gateway for the inclusion of EU principles to the Czech legal system.

In this view, Czech constitution does not determine the mechanisms of internal application but only enables that already settled principles to get inside the national system and to blossom there. Once Czech legal system was opened to the EU law, the possibility of conflict between it and national law became plausible. We must state here that Czech Constitution lacks any direct determinant of the relationship between EU and national law. In order to resolve this constitutional vacuum, the CCC had to provide some interpretations. It used the carriage of Sugar Quotas case as a historical opportunity and drew the lines of the relations between EU and Czech law. It is worth to mention here that CCC continued in pro-European reasoning. As mentioned above, the CCC acknowledged the ability of the supranational system to determine the conditions of internal application of its norms autonomously. Second, it refused its own capacity to evaluate the validity of supranational norms.[5] And besides that, CCC (being aware of the need to limit national law in favour of effective functioning of the EU) accepted also the principle of primacy as another characteristic feature of the EU law penetrating into the Czech legal system via the 'opening' clause in article 10a of the Constitution.

Although CCC accepted the penetration of EU law very widely, it was cautious about recognition of primacy as absolute and unconditional principle as claimed by the Court of Justice in case *Internationale Handelsgesellschaft*.[6] And finally it took a position which is in a line with the practice which Robert Schütze determines as a relative acceptation of the primacy principle at the national level (Schütze 2012). The arguments of CCC against the absolute meaning of primacy were based on the mechanism of transfer of competences. CCC did not consider this transfer as being unlimited. On the contrary, it based its reasoning on the concept of 'conditional conferral' and stated that: '[…]the delegation of a part of the powers of national organs may persist only so long as these powers are exercised in a manner that is compatible with the preservation of the foundations of state sovereignty of the Czech Republic, and in a manner which does not threaten the very essence of the substantive law-based state. […]'[7] CCC wagged a warning finger and reminded that the transfer of competences is not definite and unconditional. Contrary to that, possibility to confer some original competences of the Czech Republic is limited by the necessity to protect some elementary values of the Czech constitutional system—its substantive heart. CCC hence allowed for a leeway to prevent the

[5]Similar negative attitude towards possibility legality review on connection with EU law was adopted by the Polish Trybunał Konstytucyjny. This court in its judgement of 31 April 2004, K 15/04 *on participation of foreigners in European Parliamentary elections* rejected the possibility to evaluate the conformity of EU legal institute with the Polish Constitution. According to Tribunals view the Constitution could be applied only to relationships it regulates, i.e. not outside the Polish state.

[6]Internationale Handelsgesellschaft mbH vs. Einfuhr und Vorratsstelle für Getreide und Futtermittel, 11/70, ECLI:EU:C:1970:114.

[7]Sugar Quotas III, Pl.ÚS 50/04, ECLI:CZ:US:2006:Pl.US.50.04.

application (be it direct or indirect via national implementing measures or interpretation) of EU law that would be in contradiction to those inviolable principles (Maršálková 2006).

The 'so-long-as' approach of the CCC is clearly inspired by the case law of its German Counterpart. German FCC also accepts the internal application of EU law only in conditional mode and leaves the open door for the scrutinizing whether EU regulation does not affect the German standards of protection of fundamental rights or German national identity.[8]

CCC repeatedly accentuated its 'so-long-as' attitude in its rulings concerning the Treaty of Lisbon. It observed that openness and positive attitude towards the autonomy of EU law did not deprive its own role as last arbiter and a guardian of the activities of EU institutions (Zemánek 2010). But its argumentation in comparison to the Sugar Quotas case went a bit further. CCC stated that it is prepared to '[…] function as an ultima ratio and may review whether any act of Union bodies exceeded the powers that the Czech Republic transferred to the European Union under article 10a of the Constitution […]'.[9] These words (repeated in its ruling for several times) clearly demonstrate the shift toward broader limitation of EU law dominance.

According to that position, CCC may not serve only as the guarantor of the untouchable substantive heart of the Constitution (the principles which are even out of the discretion of the Czech legislator and therefore could not be transferred on supranational level) but additionally it may serve also as supervisor of the conduct of EU institutions within the fields where they embrace the legislative capacity. Once more the inspiration came from the case law of FCC which introduced the 'ultra vires' test in its Maastricht decision. Thus the option of scrutinizing the EU norms broaden from let us say substantive constitutional review (resolving the potential clashes between EU norms and core constitutional values, crossing the line of the supra-constitutional ideals and some meta-legal spheres—sovereignty, identity, rule of law, etc.) to more formal, technical review (evaluation the content and scope of EU norms vis-á-vis content and scope of conferred competences). In the first case, CCC could be able to refuse the EU rule simply because even national legislative action would be inadmissible here. In later case, CCC could be able to refuse the EU rule because it covers the question which was not conferred to the EU (yet).

Hence, the first Lisbon ruling confirmed that the effects of EU law were accepted in the Czech Republic with reservation. Simultaneously, a question was raised about the content of this reservation. Previous key rulings of CCC[10] were not clear

---

[8]FCC decision of 29 May 1974, BVerfGE 37, 271 (Solange I) Internationale Handelsgesellschaft mbH vs. Einfuhr—und Vorratstelle für Getreide und Futtermittel; FCC decision of 22 October 1986, BVerfGE 73, 339 (Solange II) Re Wünsche Handelsgesellschaft; FCC decision of 12 October 1993, BVerfGE 89, 155 Maastricht-Urteil; FCC Decision of 30 June 2009 Rozhodnutí 2 BvE 2/08 Lissabon-Urteil.

[9]Treaty of Lisbon I, Pl. ÚS 19/08, ECLI:CZ:US:2008:Pl.US.19.08.1, point 120.

[10]Sugar Quotas III, Pl.ÚS 50/04, ECLI:CZ:US:2006:Pl.US.50.04; European Arrest Warrant, Pl. ÚS 66/04, ECLI:CZ:US:2006:Pl.US.66.04.

what exactly CCC considered as the basic values of the Czech constitutionality, which it should protect. CCC only generally stated that the protected values were the Czech Republic's sovereignty, the substance of material rule of law and constitutive requirements of a democratic law abiding state. The Lisbon ruling was in this respect a substantial shift because CCC provided at least a demonstrative list (Zemánek 2009) and as such indicated that part of the material core had to be considered '[…] the principle of undeniable, inalienable, imprescriptible and irrevocable fundamental rights and freedoms of individuals, equal in dignity and rights; for the protection of which a system was built that rests on the principles of democracy, popular sovereignty, separation of powers, respecting mainly the aforementioned material conception of law abiding state'.[11]

CCC itself admitted that the definite content could be defined differently, more precisely and extensively, but it itself rejected the possibility to provide one 'academic' enumeration ruling. It stated that it has itself: '[…] many times […] declared the necessity to intensively protect principles which form the so called material core of the Constitution, but their specific enumeration is not listed in any constitutional regulation or any Constitutional Court's finding. The Constitutional Court still does not desiderate to create such enumeration decision or catalogue; such attempt would probably be appropriate if the Constitutional Court chose for its decision only the material core as a benchmark, because it would not assess a specific limited problem but an extensive aggregate of amended EU primary law and, therefore, it would be necessary to more explicitly identify what is this aggregate compared to and what not (meaning with which remaining parts of the constitutional order) […]'.[12]

The second Lisbon finding also did not bring a list of values which formed the material core of the Constitution. Due to the plaintiff's specific request, the Court had to cope with the issue of limiting EU competences and with the issue of basic requirements for the employment of EU legal instruments, i.e. the manifestations of applying these competences. In other words, it should have again focused on a further determination of the basic values of the Czech constitutional order, i.e. try to lay down the content of article 1 paragraph 1 and article 9 paragraph 2 Constitution, which in its dominant line of reasoning represented nontransferable and inviolable attributes of the Czech constitutionality and as such limited the applicability of EU law.[13] CCC refused to specify the limits of the competence transfer to the EU arguing that in this case it was a matter outside of its sphere of competence. In the Court's view, it was a political question which should have been resolved by an a priori decision of the legislature and not defined a posteriori in a judicial practice. CCC refused to articulate academic statements, i.e. to 'formulate in advance, in an abstract context, what is the precise content of Article 1(1) of the Constitution'.[14]

[11]Treaty of Lisbon I, Pl. ÚS 19/08, ECLI:CZ:US:2008:Pl.US.19.08, point 93.

[12]Treaty of Lisbon I, Pl. ÚS 19/08, ECLI:CZ:US:2008:Pl.US.19.08.1, point 93.

[13]The basis for this argumentation was laid down in the the CCC ruling Sugar Quotas III, Pl.ÚS 50/04, ECLI:CZ:US:2006:Pl.US.50.04.

[14]Treaty of Lisbon II, Pl. ÚS 29/09, ECLI:CZ:US:2009:Pl.US.29.09.3, point 112.

In its own words, it 'The Constitutional Court believes that it is specific cases that can provide it a relevant framework in which it is possible, case by case, to interpret more precisely the meaning of the term "sovereign, unitary and democratic state governed by the rule of law, founded on respect for the rights and freedoms of the man and of citizens". [...] This does not involve arbitrariness, but, on the contrary, restraint and judicial minimalism, which is perceived as a means of limiting the judicial power in favour of political processes, and which outweighs the requirement of absolute legal certainty [...] The attempt to define the term "sovereign, unitary and democratic state governed by the rule of law, founded on respect for the rights and freedoms of the man and of citizens" once and for all would, in contrast, be seen as an expression of judicial activism, which is, incidentally, consistently criticized by certain other political figures.'[15]

In the chapter, evaluating the constitutional limits of the application of EU law in the Czech Republic, one cannot exclude the controversial decision from January 2012 in Slovak pensions case (titled also as *Holubec* case).[16] In this case, CCC used its 'reservation to review' the EU norms, which was introduced in its previous case law and for the first time materially scrutinized the act of EU institution (this time the decision of the Court of Justice). And moreover it found the act of EU institution being ultra vires. But let us start with the short introduction on the circumstances of the case. In the past years, CCC repeatedly stood up for the claims of Czech citizens, who were employed by an employer based in Slovak part of former federation, to receive a compensation payment up to the level of their hypothetical pension, which they would have been entitled to once they had worked in Czech part of common state. CCC introduced this compensation supplement scale as a reaction to the unjust consequences of the exceptional historical event—the dissolution of Czechoslovakia. According to the settled practice, only Czech citizens residing in the Czech territory were entitled to this special financial supplement. However after accession of the Czech Republic to the EU, this practice entered into the Conflict with EU law requirements. It was claimed to be against the EU regulation on the coordination of social schemes, EU free movement rules and principle of non-discrimination on the basis of nationality. After series of national judicial tensions and conflicts between social security authorities, ordinary courts and CCC the question finally reached the Court of Justice as the preliminary question referred by the Supreme Administrative Court (Stehlík et al. 2014). Court of Justice in its judgement *Landtová* case[17] ruled that aforementioned special compensation was in breach with EU requirements. The main problem was its discriminatory nature. Court of Justice did not reject the supplement as such but only practice which reserved it solely to the Czech nationals residing in the territory of the Czech Republic. Its opinion clearly did not oppose the endeavour of CCC to minimalize the social injustice connected with the split of Czechoslovakia (which I

[15]Treaty of Lisbon II, Pl. ÚS 29/09, ECLI:CZ:US:2009:Pl.US.29.09.3, point 113.

[16]Slovak Pensions XVII, PL. ÚS 5/12, ECLI:CZ:US:2012:Pl.US.5.12.1.

[17]Landtová, C-399/09, ECLI:EU:C:2011:415.

believe was the main reason for the introduction of compensation supplement). Even the Luxemburg decision was 'mediatory' enough, it did not mean the end of story. In another case, the question of entitlement for the pension supplement once more reached the CCC. And CCC in its verdict from January 2012 refused the view of Court of Justice and proclaimed the ruling in *Landtová* case as ultra vires decision. In the view of CCC the question of Slovak pensions was totally outside the scope of EU law and therefore beyond the competence of the Luxemburg court. According to CCC the situations covered by the compensation scheme lack the foreign element as they were introduced as reaction on the exceptional historical event—the dissolution of Czechoslovakia where unitary social security system was used. CCC strongly blamed the Court of Justice for ignoring these historical circumstances and for ignorance of its own arguments and views. The very controversial findings of the CCC were based more on the emotional assumption than on the precise legal reasoning. There are plenty of commentaries which point on the gaps in the argumentation which I will not repeat at this place. Just to summarize: Zbíral blames the 'very poor knowledge of EU law' (Zbíral 2012); Komárek criticizes CCC for its uncooperative nature (Komárek 2012) or Bobek points on the side incentives of the CCC: 'Holubec is an odd case about judicial weariness and judicial ego' (Bobek 2014). Even though *Holubec* decision gave rise to some doubts about destruction of the subtile equilibrium settled between Luxemburg court and national authorities—labelled as 'cold war' between courts, where nobody is seriously willing to use the 'weapons of mass destruction' but time to time shows them as the potential threat. (Weiler and Haltern 1996), its weak argumentation, emotional rather than rational nature and minimal reaction of the European institutions finally led to the calm assumptions, that the war between courts did not occur yet. And besides that, the Slovak pensions question seems to be the closed chapter because in the meantime the problem (with the discrimination) was resolved by the Czech legislator by adoption of new law. Let us leave aside the question whether *Holubec* case was the rightly chosen vehicle for the CCC to get into the EU law textbooks. For the purpose of this paper, this case serves as a message that the 'so-long-as' attitude is not just an academic statement but it may occur in real cases. It proved the claim that CCC stands as a final arbiter and therefore it as a guarantor of our state sovereignty.

5.2 Constitutional Limits to the Indirect Effect of EU Law

The up-to-date case law of the CCC displayed openness and will to accept all categories of effects and consequences of EU law in the national legal system. We can say the same about the acceptance of the so-called indirect effect of EU law. The approach of the CCC towards the acceptation of the duty of EU-consistent interpretation shall be described as very open and has its origin even in the pre-accession period. CCC accepted the EU law as source of inspiration and expressed good will to seek for EU-consistent interpretation in several decisions prior to 1 May 2004.[18] It is worth to mention here, that CCC accepted EU law as important guideline for its decisions voluntarily, because before accession Czech Republic was not committed to follow the loyalty principle. I see this as another example of unprecedented dominance of EU law in the European legal space.

The crucial developments of CCC approach towards principle of EU-consistent interpretation of national law were drawn up in its seminal 'European' decisions of 2006—*Sugar Quotas* and *European Arrest Warrant* cases.[19] In the course of a few months, CCC presented answers to the questions about how it would approach this principle, which part of EU law it would consider as a model for interpretation of national law and vice versa, which part of Czech law it would open to a pro-European bending. It focuses further also on the question what are (not only constitutional) limits of application of indirect effect of EU law in national practice.[20]

In the first of the abovementioned rulings, the CCC agreed that '[it cannot] entirely overlook the impact of Community law on the formation, application, and interpretation of national law, all the more so in a field of law where the creation, operation, and aim of its provisions is immediately bound up with Community law. In other words, in this field the Constitutional Court interprets constitutional law

[18]Sanctioning of the competitors for abusing the dominant position on market, III. ÚS 31/97, ECLI:CZ:US:1997:3.US.31.97; Milk Quotas, Pl. ÚS 5/01, ECLI:CZ:US:2001:Pl.US.5.01.

[19]Sugar Quotas III, Pl.ÚS 50/04, ECLI:CZ:US:2006:Pl.US.50.04; European Arrest Warrant, Pl. ÚS 66/04, ECLI:CZ:US:2006:Pl.US.66.04.

[20]Abovementioned decisions describe the main contours of the approach of CCC towards the principle of indirect effect of EU law, but they cannot be understood as rare examples. CCC uses indirect effect quite frequently. This method of work with EU law influence was used in many cases, including the ones with big constitutional relevance. Here are some examples:

- *Burden of proof in discrimination disputes*, Pl. ÚS 37/04, ECLI:CZ:US:2006:Pl.US.37.04. Here CCC rejected the proposal to revoke provision of the Civil Procedure Code (§ 133a/2) which deals with the so-called reverse burden of proof for alleged contradiction with the right to a due process established in the Czech constitutional order. CCC claimed that national constitutional rules must be understood and interpreted with respect to the goals of the EU, its value framework and supranational system of human rights protection. Based on this, it accepted the institution of reverse burden of proof as a legitimate goal of the EU, which does not contradict our constitutional order (Matochová 2009).
- *Protection of the principle of trust in the contract relations*, II. ÚS 3/06, ECLI:CZ:US:2007:2. US.3.06.1, where CCC accented the duty of general courts to consider the value impact of EU law also in cases of legal relationships which emerged prior to accession to the EU and even before the adoption of the EU legislation, which introduced the legal rules in question. Opinion of the CCC gets ahead of the Court of Justice case law, which does not require such retroactive application of EU law principles (Ynos, C-302/04, ECLI:EU:C:2006:9).
- *State liability for damages caused by violation of EU law*, IV. ÚS 1521/10, ECLI CZ: US:2011:4.US.1521.10.1, where CCC considered the principle of a state's liability as a special autonomous liability regime valid in the Czech Republic, despite the absence of an explicit national legislation defining the process of prosecuting liability caused by the violation of EU law by a state. The acknowledgement of 'state liability principle' as legal institution which must be accepted by national courts was based on the pro-European bending of Czech national rules (Komárek 2011).

taking into account the principles arising from Community law.'[21] The most important outcome of quoted opinion is the fact that CCC accepted the impacts of indirect effect even in connection with national constitutional law. This approach brought significant consequences in the second seminal decision in *European Arrest Warrant* case. CCC described the duty of EU-consistent interpretation of national law as a constitutional principle that must be followed even by the Constitutional Court itself. According to CCC this constitutional principle 'can be derived from Art. 1 par. 2 of the Constitution, in conjunction with the principle of cooperation laid down in Art. 10 of the EC Treaty, according to which domestic legal enactments, including the constitution, should be interpreted in conformity with the principles of European integration and the cooperation between Community and Member State organs. If the Constitution, of which the Charter of Fundamental Rights and Basic Freedoms forms a part, can be interpreted in several manners, only certain of which lead to the attainment of an obligation which the Czech Republic undertook in connection with its membership in the EU, then an interpretation must be selected with supports the carrying out of that obligation, and not an interpretation which precludes it.'[22]

The up-to-date case law makes it clear that CCC adopted broad approach to the indirect effect. We may conclude that CCC considers all national norms (including constitutional level) as 'EU-consistently bendable' and reflects also itself as an addressee of the obligation to follow the EU-consistent reading of national law. EU-consistent reading of constitutional law represents an easy and effective tool for the elimination of potential contradictions between the demands of EU law and the demands of the Czech constitutional order. The relevance of this approach is significant mainly because indirect effect works as a preventive tool eliminating the 'hard' strains between EU law and national norms. Even though there might be some tensions between demands of EU law and national law in case of using the EU-consistent interpretation, the conflict is only putative. Legal contradictions which can be settled by interpretation are only a seeming one. Only contradictions which are not removable by interpretation bring as before a true normative conflict (Kysela 2009).

Case law of the CCC clearly indicates that a EU-consistent interpretation is the most ideal tool in meeting the Czech Republic's membership obligations. But it is simultaneously a tool for preserving the autonomy of the national authorities applying law, and reduces possible tensions between supranational and nation law. Furthermore, a quantitative view tells us that the phenomenon of indirect effect of EU law is in comparison with a direct applicability of the EU norms a more distinctive characteristic of supranational legal system. The approach of CCC shows that it understands this principle as a necessary component of 'everyday' practice of general courts, and not as some ultimate solution for a situation when the courts reach a dead end in their interpretations. Also, we need to mention that the

[21]Sugar Quotas III, Pl.ÚS 50/04, ECLI:CZ:US:2006:Pl.US.50.04.

[22]European Arrest Warrant, Pl. ÚS 66/04, ECLI:CZ:US:2006:Pl.US.66.04, point 61.

application of a EU-consistent reading is defined broadly in both subject (relates to all components of the Czech Republic's legal system including constitutional law) and time matter (its use excludes neither relationships nor fact situations which emerged, or rather set in, before EU accession).

Even though the principle indirect effect obviously plays an important role in the case law of CCC and is brought up relatively often, it does not mean that CCC uses it by hook or by crook. On the contrary, CCC has defined some limitations of the EU-consistent interpretation of national law, partly inspired by Court of Justice case law, partly introduced by its own. According to the CCC the norms of Czech constitutional law cannot be bent by interpretation in a biased or voluntarist way. Thus, in cases when the methodology of law interpretation does not offer any suitable method, it will not be possible to reach the expected aims of EU law. Therefore the indirect effect of EU law is limited by potential nonexistence of a national interpretation method (and on a constitutional level by the existence of the method of interpreting constitutional law) suitable for reaching the goals anticipated by EU law. Here the view of the CCC is fully compatible with the position of the Court of Justice, which takes into account the principle of national procedural autonomy and does not request national courts to meet EU goals by an absurd or fictitious reading of national law. The principle of indirect effect should be applied only within the limits of national court's discretion as established by national law. The obligation to apply EU-consistent interpretation does not mean that the reading of constitutional norms must always be in a line with the EU law requirements. It is limited by the content and systemic logic of the constitutional text. In this context CCC stated that: 'The constitutional principle that national law shall be interpreted in conformity with the Czech Republic's obligations resulting from its membership in the European Union is limited by the possible significance of the constitutional text. Article 1 par. 2 of the Constitution is thus not a provision capable of arbitrarily modifying the significance of any other express constitutional provision whatsoever.'[23] It is clear that CCC admits a pro-European reading only to the extent which is allowed by the logical content of the national constitutional norm. The more general (and therefore more flexible) the rule of the constitutional law is, the possibility of its EU-consistent interpretation is bigger. That happened to be the case in relation to the article 14 paragraph 4 second sentence of the Czech Charter of Fundamental Rights and Freedoms[24] interpreted in *European arrest warrant* case. It is so general and abstract that it gave CCC a space for a pro-European interpretation. Nevertheless, in case of strict rules which do not offer the space for interpretative manoeuvres, the principle of indirect effect of EU law cannot be applicable. In this situation the current form of the constitutional text must be respected and preferred. Under these conditions there is only one way how to meet the obligations stemming from the EU membership. It is a change of that part of

[23]European Arrest Warrant, Pl. ÚS 66/04, ECLI:CZ:US:2006:Pl.US.66.04, point 82.

[24]Article 14 paragraph 4 second sentence of the Convention says that 'No citizen may be forced to leave its homeland'.

Constitution which prevents the fulfilment of the Czech Republic's commitment to loyalty to the EU. According to the CCC, 'If the national methodology for the interpretation of constitutional law does not enable a relevant norm to be interpreted in harmony with European Law, it is solely within the Constituent Assembly's prerogative to amend the Constitution.'[25] CCC realizes here the importance of meeting the integration goals and prefers 'to adopt a European normative approach' (Gruszczak et al. 2006) in cases where the national constitutional text impedes the employment of these goals. Here we are facing another specific impact of dominance of EU law. Apart from the role of EU law as an interpretation guideline, it can also serve as a legislative incentive to adopt changes or modifications to the national Constitution. However this incentive is not unlimited. CCC repeats that the fulfilment of the Czech Republic's obligations stemming from its EU membership cannot lead to derogation of the inviolable core of the Czech Constitution. CCC states that constituent authority can decide to modify the Constitution '[...] only under the condition that it preserves the essential attributes of a democratic law-based state (Art. 9 par. 2 of the Constitution), which are not within its power to change, and not even a treaty pursuant to Art. 10a of the Constitution can assign the authority to modify these attributes [...]'.[26] The so-called 'Solange' concept of the CCC (introduced in *Sugar Quotas*[27] case), by which CCC accepts the effects of EU with reservation of non-violation of core constitutional values, applies also in this respect.

References

Bobek, M. (2014). Landtova, Holubec, and the problem of an uncooperative court: Implications for the preliminary rulling procedure. *EuConst, 10*(1), 54–89.

Gruszczak A. et al. (2006). European arrest warrant—Achievements and dilemmas. *European centre—Natolin working paper, no. 3/2006.*

Klokočka, V. (2006). *Ústavní systémy evropských států [The constitutional systems of European states].* Praha: Linde.

Komárek, J. (2011). Ústavní soud České republiky: Odpovědnost státu za škodu způsobenou porušením práva EU. [Czech constitutional court: State liability for damages caused by Breach of EU Law]. *Právní rozhledy, 19*(9), 331–335.

Komárek, J. (2012). Czech constitutional court playing with matches: The Czech constitutional court declares a judgment of the court of justice of the EU ultra vires; Judgment of 31 January 2012, Pl. ÚS 5/12, Slovak pensions XVII. *European Constitutional Law Review, 8*(2), 323–337.

Kysela, J. (2009). Mezinárodní smlouvy podle čl. 10a po 'lisabonském nálezu' Ústavního soudu [International treaties under article 10a after Lisbon decision of the constitutional court]. In A. Gerloch & J. Wintr (Eds.), *Lisabonská smlouva a ústavní pořádek ČR* [Treaty of Lisbon and the constitutional order of the Czech Republic] (pp. 49–61). Plzeň: Aleš Čeněk.

---

[25]European Arrest Warrant, Pl. ÚS 66/04, ECLI:CZ:US:2006:Pl.US.66.04, point 82.

[26]European Arrest Warrant, Pl. ÚS 66/04, ECLI:CZ:US:2006:Pl.US.66.04, point 82.

[27]Sugar Quotas III, Pl.ÚS 50/04, ECLI:CZ:US:2006:Pl.US.50.04.

Maršálková, Z. (2006). Jak daleko sahá omezení pravomocí orgánů ČR po vstupu do EU ve světle nálezu Ústavního soudu ve věci cukerných kvót [Where lay the limits of competencies of the Czech public bodies after accession to the EU in the light of CCC decision in sugar quotas case?]. *Právní rozhledy,14*(15), 553–561.

Matochová, S. (2009). Právo Evropské unie a Evropských společenství v judikatuře Ústavního soudu ČR [EC and EU law in the case law of the Czech constitutional court]. In J. Malíř el al. (Eds.), *Česká republika v Evropské unii (2004–2009). Institucionální a právní otázky členství* [Czech Republic in the EU (2004–2009). Institutional and legal aspects of membership] (pp. 29–30). Praha: Ústav státu a práva AV ČR.

Prechal, S. (2007). Direct effect, indirect effect, supremacy and the evolving constitution of the European Union. In C. Barnard (Ed.), *The fundamentals of EU law revisited. Assesing the impact of the constitutional debate* (pp. 35–69). Oxford: Oxford University Press.

Sadurski, W. (2006). 'Solange, chapter 3': Constitutional courts in Central Europe—Democracy—European Union. *EUI working paper law no.* 40.

Schütze, R. (2012). *European constitutional law*. Cambridge: Cambridge University Press.

Stehlík, V., et al. (2014). *Unijní právo před českými soudy [EU law before Czech courts]*. Praha: Leges.

Večeřa, M. & Machalová, T. (2010). *Evropeizace práva v právně teoretickém kontextu. Výklad základních pojmů* [Europeanisation of the law in the context of theory of law] Brno: Masarykova Univerzita.

Walker, N. (2007). Europe at 50—A mid-life crisis? 'Democratic Deficit' and 'Sovereignty Surplus'. *Mario Einaudi center for international studies working paper series no.* 11.

Weiler, J. H. H. & Haltern, U. (1996). The autonomy of the community legal order—Through the looking glass. *The jean monnet working paper no. 10/1996.*

Zbíral, R. (2012). Czech constitutional court, judgment of 31 January 2012, Pl. ÚS 5/12. A legal revolution or negligible episode? Court of justice decision proclaimed ultra vires. *Common Market Law Review, 49*(4), 1475–1492.

Zemánek, J. (2009). Meze ústavní autonomie EU a členských států [The boundaries of autonomy of the EU and member states]. In Z. Witkowski et al. (Eds.), *Konstytucionalyzm czeski i polski 15 i 11 lat po uchwaleniu konstytucji obu państw* [Czech and polish constitutionalism 15 and 11 Years after adoption of respective constitutions of both states] (p. 139). Toruń: WN UMK.

Zemánek, J. (2010). A European mandate of the Czech constitutional court. In H. Koch et al. (Eds.), *Europe. The new legal realism. Essays in honour of Hjalte Rasmussen* (pp. 829–844). Copenhagen: DJØF Publishin.

Chapter 6
State as a 'Creator and Master'

6.1 To Be a 'State-Like' Does not Mean to Be a State

It is clear enough that in the process of European integration Member States still figure as important players. Even the presence of defiance of the features which strengthen the EU and give it some state-like nature (Procházka 2005) the EU as a state (federation) was not ultimately established. The 'final' step is just and only in the hands of its Member States. The self-regulating ability of the EU is not unlimited. On the contrary, the activities of the EU and the effects of its law are conditioned by the existence of a national base as found in the Czech constitutional order in article 10a Constitution. It is the pouvoir constituant of all Member States and not the EU itself that holds the right to decide over the sum of competences which should be conferred to the EU (Kysela 2008). On account of this, the states are still responsible for the moderating the nature of the EU (Zemánek 2009a).

In relation to above-mentioned claims, CCC pointed to the fact that even after the big Lisbon reform it should still hold true that 'the legislative competence—competence, i.e. the authorization to amend fundamental regulations, remains with the member states. This is closely tied to the doubts of the Senate and the president concerning the character of the EU as a federal state, or the classification of powers that, according to the Senate and the president, such a state is to point out; we can briefly draw from this that if the Union does not have the competence-competence, it cannot be considered either a kind of federal state or special entity, standing in every respect and always above the individual states. The Union can act only within the scope of powers expressly conferred on it by member states, which it cannot exceed, nor can it establish new powers for itself. article 5 par. 2 of the Treaty on EU provides: "Under the principle of conferral, the Union shall act only within the limits of the competences conferred upon it by the Member States in the Treaties to

O. Hamuľák, *National Sovereignty in the European Union*,
SpringerBriefs in Law, DOI 10.1007/978-3-319-45351-4_6

attain the objectives set out therein. Competences not conferred upon the Union in the Treaties remain with the Member States. [...].'"[1]

The European Union even though it is a supranational organization it does not absorb its Member States. Those are still sovereign subjects and they serve as the foundation stones of the European Union—which is still their product. The principle of sincere cooperation (principle of loyalty) included in the article 4 paragraph 3, forms the groundwork of the Union's functioning. It is because under this principle both Union and Member States help each other in fulfilment of integrations tasks.

6.2 On the Masters of the Treaties and Beyond

The crucial element in defining the position of the Member States is connected with their functions within the Treaty revision processes. The primary EU law is with not doubt a result of an agreement between Member States. The Member States have the main responsibility for its amendment and revisions. Considering this fact they are often designated as 'Masters of the Treaties'. A procedure of revision of the primary legislation is governed by the article 48 TEU. There are two main revision procedures[2] to amend or change the text of Treaties and in both of them Member States play the crucial role.

The ordinary revision procedure is a general form of a Treaty revision and it shall be used if the objective of modification is to change significantly the content of the primary law. The competences conferred upon the Union may be both extended and reduced by this procedure. This procedure may be initiated by the government of any Member State, the European Parliament or the Commission. The proposal is submitted to the Council which postpones the proposal to the European Council. The European Council decides about a proposal by a simple majority after the consultation with the European Parliament and the Commission. In case of the adoption of the positive decision, the President of the European Council convenes the Convention, a special body whose task is to consider the proposal and carry out the consensual text of amendment to the primary law (the Convention may not be convened in case of marginal amendments). After the Convention reaches a consensus and adopts particular recommendations, the President of the Council convenes a conference of representatives of the governments of the Member States where the text of the amending Treaty to the primary law is adopted. The amendments shall enter into force after being ratified by all the Member States.

[1]Treaty of Lisbon I, Pl. ÚS 19/08, ECLI:CZ:US:2008:Pl.US.19.08.1, point 132.

[2]Which are further divided to separate modalities: ordinary procedure including Convention, ordinary procedure without Convention, simplified procedure related to internal policies of the EU and simplified procedure related to legislative processes in the EU (Denza 2013).

The simplified revision procedures shall be used for less important issues. The Treaty governs two subcategories of the simplified revision procedure. Procedure under article 48 (6) includes revisions of all or part of the provisions of Part Three of the Treaty on the Functioning of the European Union relating to the internal policies and the action of the Union. Considering the wide range of questions potentially touched by this procedure a significant restriction was introduced. According to this restriction, the simplified procedure may not lead to the extension of competences conferred upon the European Union by the Member States. Amendments should thus concern organizational and institutional issues or lead to certain clarifications, etc. The government of any Member State, the European Parliament or the Council may submit amendments under this procedure. The European Council decides about these amendments unanimously after the consultation with the European Parliament and the Commission (the European Central Bank in the case of institutional changes in the monetary area). The decision shall enter into force after approval by all Member States made under their internal constitutional rules. The second category of amendments under article 48(7) TEU contains a so-called general passerelle clause. In accordance with this clause, the European Council (by unanimous decision) may change the provisions of the TFEU which provide for the Council to act by unanimity in a given area in a manner that for the future, qualified majority in that area shall be used (this cannot be used in connection with decisions with military implications or those in the area of defence). The same may apply to all provisions of the TFEU that require a special legislative procedure for adoption of a secondary law acts. Here the European Council shall decide that in the future an ordinary legislative procedure shall be used instead. Any initiative within this procedure shall be submitted to the national parliaments. Any of them has the right to manifests its opposition within the six months period. In case of objections this procedure of the Treaty revision shall be stopped (this right to prevent the adoption of the revision of Treaties by national parliaments is designated as a 'red card' mechanism). In case when no opposition has been made, the European Council could by the unanimous decision and with the consent of the European Parliament adopt proposed change of the primary law. It is important to mention here that simplified revision procedures fall under the scrutiny of Court of Justice (De Witte and Beukers 2013). Although changes of primary law in general cannot be reviewed by the Luxembourg Court here the Court reserved itself a right to have control over procedural and formal aspects of revision.[3]

When we look on both variations of the Treaty revision processes it is clear that position of the Member States (their particular bodies) if ultimate notwithstanding the efforts to move a responsibility for at least simple amendments to the supranational level. Member States individually still possess the right of veto (in active or passive mutation) to any proposed change (Bříza 2009). As the CCC rightly stated:

[3]See judgment of the Courtof Justice of 27 November 2012, C-370/12 Pringle, ECLI:EU:C:2012:756.

'[…] The system of amending primary law, as enshrined by the Treaty of Lisbon, is proof that all the named international treaties remain such treaties even as regards revision of them, and therefore the European Union, even after the Treaty of Lisbon enters into force, will be a unique organization of an international law character. In a federative state, it is primarily up to the federal bodies to adopt amendments of the constitution; the member states of a multi-member federation, if they even take part in such a constitutional amendment, need not all agree with a constitutional amendment, and yet the amendment will enter into force. In contrast, amendment of the Treaty on EU or of the Treaty on the Functioning of the EU will be possible only with the consent of all states in the Union at an intergovernmental conference, so the role of Union bodies would be only a matter of order, not decisive; thus, Union bodies will not decide on the proposed amendments, but only organize the revision of treaties, and the amendments will enter into force after ratification by all member states in accordance with their constitutional regulations (see Art. 48 par. 1 to 5 of the Treaty on EU). Thus, even after the Treaty of Lisbon enters into force, the EU will not acquire the power to create its own new competences, the member states will still be "masters of the treaties." […]'[4]

Control over the Treaty amendments is an important sign of preservation of the sovereign position of Member States. German FCC went in this question even further than CCC. In its Lisbon decision[5] it introduced the constitutional obligation of the German bodies to perform the so-called *Integrationsverantwortung*—a permanent responsibility for the integration process. According to this constitutional obligation all proposal for the revision of the Treaties must be approved by the Act of German Parliament. This approval preserves the legitimacy chain between German demos and decisions on the European level (Grimm 2009).

The position of Member States as Masters of the Treaties is reflected also in the setting of the EU enlargement process (article 49 TEU). The interests of both the EU and its Member States are reflected in this process, which is attended by both the supranational and national institutions. The potential candidate country files a membership application with the Council, which informs the European Parliament and all national parliaments. The first decision is made at the EU level when the Council (unanimously) decides about the application upon consulting the Commission and with the assent of the European Parliament (decides by a majority of all MEPs). If the Council and the European Parliament give a positive decision, negotiation and the adoption of an accession treaty follow. The parties of this Treaty are the candidate country and the current EU Member States. Its adoption (signing the treaty) is followed by a ratification process in all Member States according to their national rules. The accession treaty enters into force after a successful ratification by all contracting parties (in current situation it would require 28 + 1 ratifications). Every Member State can veto the new member's accession on two different occasions (in the Council vote or in a national ratification). In the

[4]Treaty of Lisbon I, Pl. ÚS 19/08, ECLI:CZ:US:2008:Pl.US.19.08.1, point 146.

[5]Lisbon judgement of Federal constitutional court of 30 June 2009, 2 BvE 2/08, Absatz-Nr. 1/421.

accession process, i.e. quantitative and territorial change of the European Union, states can act as autonomous players, as sovereigns protecting their interests (geopolitical, economic and historical).

Finally, the fundamental role of states is highlighted by the emphasis on the reciprocity of integration—so-called reciprocal flexibility. This reciprocity is displayed by the explicit reference (article 48 paragraph 2 second sentence TEU), to the possibility of a negative Treaty revision in the form of reduction of EU competences (Zbíral 2015) and also in the form of introducing the possibility of Member States initiating negative legislative activity when based on the declaration no. 18 Final Act of the Intergovernmental Conference which adopted the Treaty of Lisbon, every Member State, individually or in alliance with other states, has the right to nominate the Council to ask the Commission to present a proposal for the abolition of legislation. Thus, in the area of shared competences the Member States will have received a possibility to regain a shared competence which the EU does not use or to defend its competences in case the adoption of such legislative act that violated the principles of transferred competence (Belling et al. 2010).

The Lisbon reform of primary law was based on the concept of balancing when the increase in 'federalizing element' was accompanied by reform steps increasing legitimacy of decision-making in the EU and strengthening Member States' supervision possibilities (Zemánek 2009b). Primary example of this 'counter-arrangement' is a new system for controlling, that the subsidiarity principle is observed when EU legislation is drafted by engaging the national parliaments according to Protocol (no. 2) on the application of the principles of subsidiarity and proportionality (article 4). Every proposed legislative act must be submitted to the national parliaments of all Member States. This mechanism is known as Early Warning System and serves for the observation whether the subsidiarity principle is fulfilled (Kiiver 2012). National parliaments have the possibility to express their view (in the form of the so-called reasoned opinion) on the proposed legislative act. The period for observation was set to eight weeks. In case that one-third of national parliaments[6] raises an objection to the proposal, the institution which presented it is obliged to take these objections and observations into consideration and decide if it will keep, change or withdraw the proposal (the so-called 'yellow card' objection). If at least a simple majority of national parliaments objects the Commission's proposal and the Commission upon the examination of their observation decides to keep the proposal, it must duly justify it. The positions of the national parliaments and Commission are then together with the proposal submitted to the European Parliament and Council. The EU norm maker has to take into consideration both alternative views and come to terms with submitted proposals when adopting the act (the so-called 'orange card' objection). National parliaments serve here as the protectors of constitutional balance between EU and Member States in question of division of powers. CCC realized this

[6]Each national parliament disposes of two votes: in case of two chambers, each house possesses one vote.

function and underlined the increased role of the national parliaments as the argument in favour of preserving the national sovereignty in decision in case Treaty if Lisbon I. CCC gave the emphasis on the increased function and role of national parliaments in the process of determination and control of the balance in the system of pooled sovereignty within the Europe. National parliaments as the protectors of principle of subsidiarity are obtaining the strong instrument and may become one of the most important players in the field of execution of shared competences (Auel 2007). CCC gave us clear proof of its ability of sensible anticipation of mechanisms and trends behind the European legal integration. Lisbon concept of extended powers of national parliaments gives rise to the notion of a priori control of constitutional issues and offer the space for exclusion of constitutional tenses in the stage of preparation of legislative outcomes. Inclusion of national parliaments into the group of European constitutional players gives rise to the more efficient system of cooperation and creation of multi-level constitutional system. CCC was aware of this opportunity when it stated, that: '[…] Treaty of Lisbon expands the present framework […] by including the parliaments of member states in the process of review of the exercise of competences […]. Thus, the parliaments of member states can play an important role in protecting the limits of competences which the member states conferred on the Union. […]. Review of observing the limits of the conferral of competences is thus the joint role of all participating bodies, both at the European level and at the domestic level.'[7]

6.3 The State Holds Its Destiny in Its Own Hands

The Member States are the original holders of competences and act as a Master of the Treaties but moreover they remain as independent units capable to make the own decision about their future. Their right to withdraw from the Union, which was introduced by the Treaty of Lisbon (see article 50 TEU—the so-called exit clause) underlines this fact.[8] Member States must be understood as the 'holders of their own destiny', the masters in the Schmitt's extreme situation. Carl Schmitt commences his Political Theology by famous sentence that 'sovereign is who decides on the exception' (Schmitt 1985), where exception means the stepping outside the ordinary state of things, to stand outside the legal rules. Within the supranational legal system, the Schmitt's exception means to stand outside the EU, not to be the one of the Member States. This crucial (and extreme) position is absolutely in the hands of each and every Member State, which should act as a sovereign when using the exit clause of article 50 TEU.

[7] Treaty of Lisbon I, Pl. ÚS 19/08, ECLI:CZ:US:2008:Pl.US.19.08.1, point 140.

[8] Until the Treaty of Lisbon came into effect, the EU law did not regulate explicitly the possibility of a Member State to leave the EU. The most probable reason for this silence about withdrawal seems to be the intent of the founders to dissuade Member States from withdrawal (Wyrozumska 2013). The withdrawal itself, however, was never denied by the Treaties.

Explicit regulation of the right for unilateral voluntary withdrawal from the Union apparently finished the debates whether withdrawal from the Union should be perceived from constitutional (federal) of international point of view. The federal systems usually do not permit the unilateral withdrawal without necessary change of constitution. Federations are based on the notion of indissoluble unity (Wyrozumska 2013). On the contrary, the international law perspective when dealing with the membership of the states in the international organizations or when dealing with the international treaty regimes is more open and more tolerant to the autonomy of state's will (and the state's sovereignty[9]) hence rules of international law (Vienna Convention on the Law of Treaties, 1969) allow a state to end up its commitments arising from the international treaties and analogically to end up the membership in the international organizations founded by the international treaty. Explicit regulation of the right to withdraw from the Union shifted the discussions towards later option and underlined the concept of the EU as the bound of sovereign states. CCC noticed this conceptual change and used the right to withdraw from the Union as an argument in favour of preserving the sovereignty of the Czech Republic when participating on the European integration. CCC reminded that: '[…] the Treaty of Lisbon newly introduces, in Art. 50 of the Treaty on EU, the possibility of withdrawing from the organization. This can take place by agreement between the withdrawing state and the Council as a representative of the member states (i.e., not with the Commission, as a representative of the interests of the Union itself), and if an agreement is not reached, the Treaty itself gives the withdrawing state a notice period. Thus, the manner of termination membership is also typical for an international organization, not a contemporary federative state, and this possibility, on the contrary, strengthens the sovereignty of member states. […]'[10]

A state's withdrawal from the EU has to be first of all a consensual process. A Member State wishing to withdraw notifies its intention to the European Council, which provides guidelines for the conclusion of an agreement setting out the arrangements for its withdrawal. These negotiations are on behalf of the EU conducted by a negotiator (article 218 paragraph 3 TEU) and when the negotiations are completed, the agreement is concluded on behalf of the European Union by the Council, after obtaining the consent of the European Parliament. The EU institutions can thus affect the process of a state's withdrawal, but not the withdrawal itself. Mattias Kumm labelled the participation of institutions on the withdrawal process (then according to the draft Constitutional Treaty) as a display of Europeanization of residual national sovereignty (Kumm 2005). The withdrawal agreement is not an absolute condition of membership termination. If the agreement is not agreed on or is not accepted, membership comes to an end two years after the

[9]Voluntary membership in international organizations was always seen as a basis of state sovereignty. It was the case even with the historically first global integration organization—League of Nations. Voluntary membership was also in its case the (positive) answer to the question whether states which joined an international organization and so accepted certain limitations on their sovereignty can still be seen as sovereign subjects (Le Fur 1935).

[10]Treaty of Lisbon I, Pl. ÚS 19/08, ECLI:CZ:US:2008:Pl.US.19.08.1, point 146.

Member State declared its intention to the European Council. Accession and withdrawal are autonomous rights of the states and their membership is their privilege, which cannot be taken away by a decision of an institution or a decision of other Member States—EU law does not make it possible to expel a state from the Union by the decision of others.

References

Auel, K. (2007). Democratic accountability and National parliaments: Redefining the impact of parliamentary scrutiny in EU affairs. *European Law Journal, 13*(4), 487–504.

Belling, V. et al. (2010). *Kontrola dělby pravomocí v EU se zřetelem ke kompetenčním excesům.* [Control of the division of powers within the EU with the accent on the ultra vires excesses]. Praha: Ústav státu a práva AV ČR.

Bříza, P. (2009). The Czech Republic: The constitutional court on the Lisbon treaty decision of 26 November 2008. *European Constitutional Law Review, 5*(1), 143–164.

De Witte, B., & Beukers, T. (2013). The court of justice approves the creation of the European stability mechanism outside the EU legal order: Pringle. *Common Market Law Review, 50*(3), 805–848.

Denza, E. (2013). Commentary on article 48 TEU. In H.-J. Blanke & S. Mamgiameli (Eds.), *The Treaty on European Union. A commentary*. (pp. 1331–1355). Heidelberg: Springer.

Grimm, D. (2009). Defending sovereign statehood against transforming the union into a state. *European Constitutional Law Review, 5*(1), 353–373.

Kiiver, P. (2012). *The early warning system for the principle of subsidiarity. Constitutional theory and empirical reality*. London: Routledge.

Kumm, M. (2005). To be a European citizen: Constitutional patriotism and the Treaty establishing a constitution for Europe. In E. O. Eriksen, et al. (Eds.), *The European constitution: The Rubicon crossed?* (pp. 7–63). Oslo: Arena.

Kysela, J. (2008). Lisabonská smlouva v kontextu předběžného přezkumu Ústavním soudem. [Treaty of Lisbon in the context of its preliminary review by the constitutional court] *Právní zpravodaj, 9*(6), 5.

Le Fur, L. (1935). *Nástin mezinárodního práva veřejného [Introduction to the public international law]*. Praha: Orbis.

Procházka, R. (2005). Európska únia ako štátny zväzok [EU as union of states]. *Justičná revue, 57* (1), 96–103.

Schmitt, C. (1985). *Political theology: Four chapters on the concept of sovereignty*. Cambridge, Massachusetts: The MIT Press.

Wyrozumska, A. (2013). Commentary on art. 50 TEU. In H.-J. Blanke, S. Mamgiameli (Eds.), *The treaty on European Union. A commentary*. (pp. 1385–1418). Heidelberg: Springer.

Zbíral, R. (2015). Restoring tasks from the European Union to member states: A bumpy road to an unclear destination? *Common Market Law Review, 52*(1), 51–84.

Zemánek, J. (2009a). Kompetenční a hodnotový rámec Evropské unie v 'lisabonském' nálezu Ústavního soudu [the competence and value framework of the EU in the Lisbon decision of the constitutional court]. In A. Gerloch & J. Wintr (Eds.), *Lisabonská smlouva a ústavní pořádek ČR [Treaty of Lisbon and the Czech constitutional order]* (pp. 135–147). Plzeň: Aleš Čeněk.

Zemánek, J. (2009b). Ústavní rozměr členství v Evropské Unii a otázka souladu Lisabonské smlouvy [Constitutional dimension of the membership in the EU and question of constitutionality of the treaty of Lisbon]. In J. Malíř et al. (Eds.), *Česká republika v Evropské unii (2004–2009). Institucionální a právní otázky členství*. [Czech Republic in the EU (2004–2009). Institutional and legal aspects of membership] (pp. 34–54). Praha: Ústav státu a práva AV ČR.

Chapter 7
Conclusion

European integration brings a Janus-faced dilemma. Apart from understanding states as building blocks of the EU, we must keep in mind the mixed character of the European integration project. On one hand, there is the accentuated key role of the Member States and the international legal foundation of the EU (states as sovereigns), and on the other hand there is the process of gaining independence and autonomous constitutionalization of the European Union (EU as a new sovereign).

European integration is ironic also because the consensus of political representation of its Member States on the choice of supranational form of integration and its autonomy (which is the basis for the tension between European and the national legal systems) is accompanied by theoretical disputes and the following disagreement among judicial authorities.

Conflicts within legal theory and government studies concern the extent to which new phenomena are accepted and the will to search for new meanings of classical institutes. The content of the 'dispute' between the Court of Justice and the national (mostly constitutional) courts concerns the relationship between EU law and national law and the never-ending dialogue about determining the superiority of one or the other.

The EU is a supranational organization which fulfils its own goals through the original structure of institutions (mostly independent of Member States' influence) and through their own legal tools, which form an independent and dominant legal system. On top of that, the evolution of European Communities and consequently the European Union is accompanied by the phenomenon of factual or material constitutionalization. The EU becomes a new sovereign. Its sovereignty does not in any way touch the original sovereignty of the Member States. The EU does not replace the states it is a personification of their common project. When we accept that the EU is from material, functional point of view sovereign, it does not mean that we open the space for speculations that Member States are losing their sovereignty. Member States formed a new sovereign entity, with which they share a common territory on which it executes its power. The relationship between the EU and its Member States is not connected by splitting of sovereignty but by

O. Hamuľák, *National Sovereignty in the European Union*,
SpringerBriefs in Law, DOI 10.1007/978-3-319-45351-4_7

overlapping sovereign competences of both. The Federal Constitutional Court's decision articulated in the Lisbon judgement[1] that 'state is not a myth' is not especially important. States as the original holders of competences continue to be sovereign. Their position is after the explicit stipulation that they can unilaterally leave the EU even stronger and becomes autonomous. The new EU sovereignty does not build on nothing. The states continue to be the EU's building blocks. They are though limited in order to achieve common objectives of integration.

The need to harmonize identified contradictions (a new sovereign next to old sovereigns) brings a shift in the hermeneutical dimension of sovereignty; it brings a novelty in the definition and understanding of state sovereignty. CCC dedicates its Lisbon rulings to this new understanding and offers a new, flexible approach to state sovereignty. In its view, the EU applies the concept of so-called pooled sovereignty where common goals are reached by participation of a plurality of actors. CCC understands sovereignty as a responsibility for securing a high-quality existence of society as a prerequisite for economic reproduction and reproduction of the states' value base.

Apart from hermeneutical shifts, we still have a real world of mutual relationships of various norm-making centres. And here we face the question where the relationship between the Czech and EU law affects our sovereignty. Sovereignty stands as a preservation of the basic features of national constitutionality. And in this view it could be undermined if all national law were subordinated to EU law.

CCC addresses this relationship question already in its key rulings *Sugar Quotas* and *European Arrest Warrant*.[2] Here it on one hand acknowledges the EU law as an autonomous legal system, which defines for itself its application principles. On the other hand, it recalls that the acceptance of supranational law does not mean acknowledgement of its absolute primacy over all national law.[3] CCC does not consider the delegation of competences, which is the constitutional foundation of the EU law effects in the Czech legal system, permanent and unlimited. On the contrary, it articulates a reservation which could serve as a basis for non-recognition of the effects of EU law. It addresses the Court of Justice and mainly the EU institution, a message that it does not plan to respect those results of their activities, i.e. those norms of EU law, which would be in contradiction with fundamental principles of the Czech constitutional law. CCC recalled that the European integration project had certain limits and that its self-regulating ability was not unlimited already in its first 'Lisbon' ruling. It stated that even though European integration was a positive challenge for the Czech Republic and it carried with itself enrichment of state sovereignty by new possibilities, it had (and would have) still limited character depending on its constitutional conformity.[4] Thus, it repeatedly

[1]Lisbon judgement of Federal constitutional court of 30 June 2009, 2 BvE 2/08, Absatz-Nr. 1/421.

[2]Sugar Quotas III, Pl.ÚS 50/04, ECLI:CZ:US:2006:Pl.US.50.04; European Arrest Warrant, Pl. ÚS 66/04, ECLI:CZ:US:2006:Pl.US.66.04.

[3]Sugar Quotas III, Pl.ÚS 50/04, ECLI:CZ:US:2006:Pl.US.50.04.

[4]Treaty of Lisbon I, Pl. ÚS 19/08, ECLI:CZ:US:2008:Pl.US.19.08.1.

accentuated its 'Solange' position expressed already in *Sugar Quotas* case. Hence, even though it did not find any reason for finding the Treaty of Lisbon incompatible with the Constitution of the Czech Republic, this reminder, a raised finger, met the content of its role as a guardian of the Czech constitutionality. CCC then used this raised finger again (into some extent controversial way) in its ruling *Slovak Pensions/Holubec* case,[5] where it from a purely doctrinal point of view confirmed its role of the warden of European institutions and its relative attitude to the supremacy of EU law.

When answering the question whether European integration (and the primacy of EU law over national law as one of its strongest autonomy tools) interferes with practical sovereignty of the Czech Republic, I have to (following the CCC judgements) answer no. As the Czech Republic's EU membership does not suppress inviolable attributes of the Czech constitutionality, I believe it cannot interfere with state sovereignty on a practical level because even though formally the (time unlimited) right to execute some sovereign competences is transferred to the EU, its transfer is conditioned and the results of applying these competences cannot affect basic guarantees, which this right assigns to the subjects of the Czech Republic's constitutional law.

[5]Slovak Pensions XVII, PL. ÚS 5/12, ECLI:CZ:US:2012:Pl.US.5.12.1.

FSC
www.fsc.org
MIX
Papier | Fördert gute Waldnutzung
FSC® C083411

Kolibri 360 GmbH
Ferdinand-Jühlke-Straße 7
99095 Erfurt, Deutschland
produktsicherheit@kolibri360.de